WINE-MAKING
AT HOME

WINE-MAKING AT HOME

By Bruce Palmer

Workman Publishing Company
New York

ALSO BY BRUCE PALMER

MAKING CHILDREN'S FURNITURE
AND PLAY STRUCTURES

Novels
BLIND MAN'S MARK
FLESH AND BLOOD
HORSESHOE BEND
HECATOMB
THEY SHALL NOT PASS

Short Stories
MANY ARE THE HEARTS

Children's Books
FIRST BULL RUN
CHANCELLORSVILLE

Illustrations by Jack Marmaras.
Cover photograph by Jerry Darvin
Cover design by Paul Hanson

ISBN: 0-911104-58-5

Workman Publishing Company
1 West 39 Street
New York, New York 10018

Printed and bound by the George Banta Company

Manufactured in the United States of America
Second edition
First printing April 1975

10 9 8 7 6 5 4 3

Contents

PART 2   SLIP-SKIN SQUEEZINGS

White Wine from Red Grapes
Animal Charcoal
The Master Vintner: A Dramatic Interlude

PART 3   HOME FRUIT WINES

Summer and Winter Wines
5 Gallons Each
A 10-Gallon Crock
Yeast Starters, Again
Some Hints, Cautions, and Reminders
Some "Nevers" to Know
How to "Fine" Wine
Fortifying Fruit Wines

Cider Wine
Away with Froth
Apple Wine
Drinken-Sie Deutsch?
Strainer-Bags
How Much is a Bushel?
Sugar: A Rule-of-Thumb
Master's Choice
Blueberry Wine
Measure for Measure
All's Well that Ends Well
Cherry Wine
"I Gave My Love a Cherry . . ."
Slow Stuff
Peach Wine
Cream of Tartar
Clear or Fine
Raisin Wine
Watch that H_2O

High-Rise Honey Wine
Dandelion Wine
The Dandelion Myth
Dent de Lion

Licensed Wine-Maker
Equipment List for Wine-Making
Some Chemicals Used in Wine-Making
Hand-and Electric-Powered Crushers, Wine
    Presses
Fruit Crushers and Grinders (Manufacturers)
Fruit and Cider Presses
Grape Presses
Wine-Supply Houses

Back of the wine is the vintner,
And back through the years his skill,
And back of it all are the vines in the sun
And the rain . . .and the Master's will.

Anonymous, nineteenth century

Introduction

Wine-making is one of the oldest activities of man, a happy and honorable occupation. The processing of nature's gifts in the company of family and friends is love's labor—peaceful, productive, and potable. Wine-making decants the best in grapes and fruits and the best in those who crush and cork. Press, bung, and barrel are the tools of this liquid alchemy and bring forth, in their season, good appetite for all.

It is well-known that the ancients worshipped a god of wine as a benefactor of humankind. The brimming cup and shimmering glass have long been regarded as the perfect and proper accompaniment for festivals and feasts, for religious rituals and ceremonies. The bottle on the table has consoled and cheered proletarians and potentates, philosophers and peasants. Wine warms the heart and loosens the tongue. It is the drink praised in song and poem, the wiseman's friend, the gracious gift from host to guest, the subtle ambassador between the lover and his lady, and the pledge to the groom and his bride.

A great many words have been written over the centuries about wine: learned tomes, technical volumes, arguments as bitter as last year's dregs, books written by the silly to flatter the snobbish. As much misinformation as truth has been offered in testimony to a drink that deserves to be taken seriously, but not solemnly. These pages are devoted to the *processes* of wine-making on a modest scale, not to the end product. Their purpose is to provide a concise, informative manual that will enable the interested but unskilled wine-lover to make, from wine grapes, table grapes, or local orchard fruits, a variety of superior wines at a very low cost.

The book you hold is divided into three how-to sections: FIFTY GALLONS PLUS, SLIP-SKIN SQUEEZINGS, and HOME FRUIT WINES. FIFTY GALLONS PLUS is for ambitious and thirsty oenophiles who intend to make that much American red wine from native wine grapes *(Vitis vinifera)*. SLIP-SKIN SQUEEZINGS covers methods of processing table grapes *(Vitis labrusca)* into smaller quantities of red or white wine. HOME FRUIT WINES is for the year-round experimenter who may be limited by available space, geography or pocketbook.

Why only *red* wine in bulk, when white is about equally preferred? The reason is that red wine grapes are more easily obtainable in large amounts and are less expensive to buy. The California growers of *Vitis vinifera* generally ship out of their sun-drenched state only those varieties that are suitable for making red wine. If you are thinking big, think red.

White wine fanciers can purchase *Vitis vinifera* types at the California vineyards. Pinot Chardonnet, for instance. As for *Vitis labrusca* varieties, here again grapes for red wine are more available. However, there are varieties that make good to excellent white wine—Catawba, Dela-

location and work force several months before you set out to barter for the first box of grapes or bushel of orchard fruits.

There are six steps that turn your grapes to wine. Glance through the following rundown and read on. All will be revealed.

Step One   CRUSHING. All purchased grapes must be crushed, either by hand or mechanically, in order to ensure uniform fermentation. The individual grape must have the skin broken to expose the interior pulp, which contains the sugar. It is this sugar that converts to alcohol. NEVER WASH THE GRAPES!

Step Two   FERMENTING. The crushed grapes must remain in a fermenting container, small or large, until the yeasts that are natural to the fruit have completed the process of converting the fruit sugar to alcohol. Some grapes of the *Vitis labrusca* varieties require the addition of measured amounts of sugar, plus the use of commercial yeast to ensure proper fermentation, complete conversion of sugar to alcohol and a good wine. Fermenting normally begins within twelve hours after the fruit has been crushed and lasts from five to ten days. Active fermenting of crushed grapes (and fruits) can be both seen and heard, a steady bubbling that throws off a harmless gas and converts much of the crushed pulp and skins to an opaque, sweet liquid called must.

Step Three   PRESSING. When the fermenting process is complete, the must will no longer bubble or will nearly stop. The contents of the fermenting container should be pressed, either by hand in a clean linen bag, or in a mechanical wine or fruit press. As much juice as possible should be squeezed from the fermented pulp, which can then be discarded. The liquid should be strained through a sieve or cheesecloth before being poured into the aging container.

Step Four

AGING. The strained liquid requires a period of time to finish final fermenting and to settle and clear. All containers of wood or glass must be scrupulously cleaned before use. The must will give off small amounts of harmless gas. Since exposure to the air is bad for wine, aging containers of any type must be sealed to let the gas out but prevent air from getting in. Wine made from grapes is typically aged for ninety days, then transferred to a new aging container. Small amounts of wine made from orchard fruits may be bottled as soon as they have settled and cleared.

Step Five

RACKING. Wine from grapes that has aged in wood or glass containers should be siphoned or pumped into clean containers. The thick sediment that has settled in the original containers should be discarded and the containers cleaned or purified. Since racking improves both the clarity and taste of grape wine, home vintners should rack *at least twice* before bottling. Use inexpensive cheesecloth as a filter to minimize the amount of sediment in the second racking.

Step Six

BOTTLING. Wine twice-racked is siphoned into fifth, quart, half-gallon or gallon bottles that have been very carefully washed clean with hot water. Each bottle is sealed, either with a corking device or by new screw-type closures. Never use old corks or used closures. Allow wine to settle in the bottle before drinking. Wine continues to age in the bottle and typically improves in bouquet and taste until the third year, sometimes longer.

Step-by-Step Annual Production
of 200 Fifth Bottles of Good Red Wine

FIFTY GALLONS PLUS

BARRELS, BUNGS, AND BRIMSTONE

First Steps and Initial Costs

Before you commit yourself, family, or friends to making wine by the barrel, pause a moment to consider the consequences. The first year of production is likely to cost as much as the next five years combined. (You are obliged to purchase two fifty-gallon barrels for fermenting and two more for the aging process.) You will occupy a fair-sized portion of your cellar for a calendar year. A good deal of your weekends will be spent tracking down barrels, wholesale grape dealers, a crusher, and a wine press. You are likely to neglect your lawn and put off all home repairs, and certain relatives and neighbors will think their darkest suspicions of your character confirmed. Finally, you will be obliged to deal with the Internal Revenue Service.

Weekend Wining

License and Permits

Before investing any money or time, you must write to your district I.R.S. office and obtain a license for making up to 250 gallons of wine on your premises for private consumption and not for resale. The license can be shown to all scoffers before you tack it up on the cellar wall. You are allowed, at this point, a moment of quiet pride. You have announced yourself a serious, if novice, wine-maker.

Buying Barrels

The volume of wine you have decided to make obliges you to buy barrels. But not any old barrels. What you need are four *charred oak* whiskey barrels, fifty-gallon capacity each. They are likely to cost at least ten dollars apiece. You will have to make inquiries. Start by locating the nearest bottling plant. Such firms receive spirits in barrels. Laws governing the manufacture of some whiskeys limit or prohibit reuse of barrels for the same kind of whiskey and so they are often resold for other purposes. Brandy barrels are even better than whiskey, but harder to come across. Phone or write the plant manager and ask his price. If the price is right, set a date to pick them up *no later than mid-August.*

Used, not New

Yellow-Paging

Another place to look for barrels (as well as other wine-making equipment) is in "the Italian section" of the nearest large city. Use the yellow pages to locate several food importer/wholesalers and call each, explaining your needs. Do not make any offer over the phone. The merchant on the other end may not carry barrels himself, but he will certainly know people who do, or (better) will have a relative, friend or acquaintance who makes wine in large amounts. Get *his* name and track *him* down.

What to Buy and When

Barrels obey the law of supply and demand, so you should buy in the off-season, late spring or early summer. Take your nose along when you open negotiations with any private dealer. Never buy a sealed barrel. Your barrels should each have one hole in its side. Sniff carefully. Reject any barrel that stinks. A good barrel will smell like

Sniff and Shop   wine, not herring. Ask the dealer when it was last used and what kind of wine was made. Ask him if it was "sulphured" after being emptied. Look the barrel over for signs of mold (which indicates a leak) and make certain it has at least four steel hoops. The better the barrel, the better your wine will be. Shop around. Ask for prices.

Obviously, if you buy barrels from a plant or distiller, you can take what he has with confidence. High-proof alcohol prevents the growth of mold or bacteria, and you can be certain the barrels never leaked. With private dealers, be prudent. And be prepared both to bargain and to pay in cash. If you can't locate four barrels you can purchase your two aging barrels first, at the same time snooping for fermenting (or "crushing") barrels.

By whatever means, you have now two fermenting barrels and two aging barrels. Fetch your barrels home in someone's borrowed station wagon. But before you part company with your

Get Free Info   barrel dealer, ask his advice about, and addresses for, sulphur sticks and bungs; you will need about six of each. Ask him, too, for the names, addresses, and telephone numbers of any wine-makers who might be willing to rent you a crusher and a press. Leave your own name and number. Mention the fact that you are going to make fifty gallons and are interested in the name of a reputable grape-broker or wholesaler.

**To Make
Fermenters**

Your two fermenting barrels have to be made into fermenters. If you buy them from a dealer you can probably get them previously prepared—usually for the same price or slightly less. If you buy from a bottler or distiller, you have to plug the side with a wooden bung driven home tight with a hammer and break open one end. This is hard work, since a good barrel is made of tough oak. Drill a hole and cut across with a keyhole saw several times in the same plank. Work this plank loose and knock the others out with an ax or hammer.

Making a fermenting barrel.

**Agers: Soda
and Sulphur**

Assume that no barrel is fit for your wine. Clean the open-ended fermenting barrels very carefully with warm water, an abundant amount of baking soda, and a stiff scrub brush. Rinse thoroughly and store upside down.

Mix four tablespoons of baking soda with two gallons of warm water and pour this mixture through a funnel into your two aging barrels. Seize the ends of each and rock, hard, while whistling three stanzas, with chorus, of *Drink to Me Only With Thine Eyes*. Flush the barrels out thoroughly with a garden hose and drain them. Tap a new bung into each, gently. Go get two sulphur sticks, some matches, a sharp nail, and about three feet of fine wire.

A sulphur stick is a flat, thin strip of fabric impregnated with sulphur. It is about six inches long and two inches wide. Punch a hole in one end, loop and twist the wire to hold the stick. Snip the wire in half, about eighteen inches long. Remove the bung from the washed and rinsed aging barrel, light the sulphur stick on fire. It will burn with a sputtering blue flame, the sulphur will melt and drip, and the smell will be Gawd-awful. Let it burn a minute, then lower it down inside

Sulphur Sticks Stink

the barrel and tap home the bung, leaving a six inch tail of wire sticking out. While kids are wowed by this performance, do not let them do it. Liquid sulphur can give a third-degree burn.

You should see a thin stream of foul-smelling blue smoke leak up around the bung and hear a hissing sound. The burning sulphur uses up all the oxygen and creates a slight vacuum. Wait five minutes and pry out the bung with a screwdriver, holding the wire tail with the other hand. Lift out the charred stick, which should be nearly or completely burned. Throw it away, but save the

Murder Bacteria

wire. Drive the bung back snug and store the aging barrel. You have just murdered any bacteria that lurked within and annihilated any mold capable of spoiling your wine. Sulphur your second aging barrel.

Sulphuring an aging barrel.

Soaking

Though all your barrels have been cleaned, and the two agers purified, they still have to be soaked to make them absolutely tight before they can be used. At least *two weeks before* buying grapes, roll all your barrels out into the yard and fill them full of water, both the open-ended fermenters and the bung-stopped aging barrels. Since oak staves shrink when dry, it is likely that all

How to Hop

your barrels will leak. If the staves are actually loose, drive the hoops toward the belly of each barrel with a hammer and a screwdriver. A handy system is to hoop first, then place the open-ended fermenters in a back-yard pool for about three days, rolling them around twice daily. You will ruin the kids' swimming, but it will speed up the swelling process. Fill the aging barrels with a hose, and keep them filled. Change the water *at least once*, otherwise it will stagnate, leaving an unpleasant smell and taste.

Your basic containers, two fermenters and two aging barrels, must soak and swell until they are absolutely watertight. Make sure they are so one week before buying your grapes and obtaining a crusher. Now invest a few hours to simplify the pleasant tasks that lie ahead.

The Basic Wine Cave

Ideal Cellar Temp

Any conventional cellar high enough to stand up straight in with reasonable light and no serious leaks will do. Ideally, the temperature should not go higher than sixty-five degrees at anytime of the year. Do not make wine right next to the furnace, but in a far corner, near a window that can be propped open.

Clear an area, allowing elbow room to move barrels about. (By now you have learned that empty barrels are clumsy and water-filled ones very heavy.) To insure that fermentation will be even and that no barrel will topple or spill, use heavy cinder blocks to elevate the two upright fermenting barrels and to support one of your aging barrels on its side. You will need some sturdy planking, two-by-fours or heavier, some small pieces of lumber for wedges and braces to keep the aging barrel from rolling, a hammer, and some eight-penny nails.

Braces for Barrels

The Day Before

The day before you buy your grapes, get the fermenting barrels solidly placed on their cinder-block foundations. Drain one aging barrel and leave it outdoors. Empty the other aging barrel and place it, one end against a wall and carefully braced, ready to receive the grape juice after pressing. *Sulphur this aging barrel again.* Use half of a sulphur stick, proceed as before, discard the charred remainder of the stick and bung snug. Cover the floor area with several issues of last month's Sunday newspaper.

Get Ready, Get Set

Confirm the availability of wine grapes. Make certain that a rented crusher (page 26) will be ready for you to pick up. Check the readiness of all subordinates and timetables for transportation to and from your grape wholesaler. You will need two station wagons or a pickup truck.

Read the section immediately following with great care, at least twice, committing key portions to memory and making marginal notes where you deem fit.

The Master Vintner: First Steps to Benevolent Despotism

This book is the key to *all.* Keep it ever in your possession. Let no underling, neither kith nor kin, get his hands on it. Knowledge is power.

From the first heft of the first barrel through final day-before preparations, you should be in clear command of the situation. As Master Vintner, you have negotiated the first investments of money and labor time. Your position is that of an executive. By assuming responsibility, you qualify for command. Cultivate a cool demeanor, an air of age-old wisdom. Assign to others the menial tasks they seem eager to perform, but check all scrubbing, flushing, and soaking with grave care. Perform the magic of the sulphur sticks with a casual deliberateness. Obtain a notebook, and keep records of names, addresses, telephone numbers of all barrel and equipment purveyors, grape merchants, and subordinates.

An Executive Position

Purchase a plain blue apron and, perhaps, a green eye-visor such as worn by card-dealers and telegraph operators. Be seen taking short, thoughtful walks carrying a five-foot staff. While lesser folk buzz about cutting grass and puttering on ladders, spend your time reading ahead in this book and casting quizzical glances at the sky, as though assuring yourself of prime harvest conditions.

Control Your Journeyman

Delegate subordinate positions with care. Select some strong and trustworthy person and name him (temporarily) Journeyman. His charge is the barrels: cleaning, flushing, driving the hoops down to tighten the staves, checking for leaks, making sure there are adequate bungs. Allow him to think that some day (not soon) he will be allowed to burn a sulphur stick or two.

Sorcerer's Apprentice

Be liberal, at first, in the creation of Apprentices. Bestow this rank upon lively strong men and even upon children of ten years and up. They will be grateful, even excited; in their innocence they can have no idea of the tedious labor it is their lot to perform. (While you watch.) Demonstrate first, of course, but never give any indication that you plan to complete the chore once begun. You will "show how it's done." Period. They will do it, without a lot of back-talk. Period.

Wine and Women

Wine-making has considerable appeal for active male children. It is one of the few chances that comes their way to get *really dirty* while doing something that is, beyond question, useful (if not for them). Women, as a sex, deplore mess and disorder. They have enough else to worry about so that wine-making seldom becomes their ruling passion. They make expert bottlers, however, a fact not to be forgotten. Forgive them if they have little enthusiasm for toiling with barrels, crusher, and press. No general launches an attack with auxiliary troops.

LMWMG & FDL   *La Mancha Wine-Making, Gustatory, and Folk-Dancing League* is typical of home wine-making fraternities. The Master Vintner knows everything and gives all the orders. Experience has proven that cellar work progresses better if commands are bucked down to the Journeyman who goads the Apprentices. Since all share the end product equally, the benevolent despotism of a medieval guild is a condition of cooperative labor submitted to because it works. It is also fun. And that's what wine-making is all about!

THE WRATH OF GRAPES

What the wine-maker finds available in the way of grapes depends on his geographical location. This geographical location also affects their cost. A Californian will have a greater choice than a Tennessee wine-maker and his grapes will cost him less. In the last decade, the cost of grapes has doubled. Many home wine-makers are seeking

Look for Local Grapes

vineyards closer to them, rather than paying for Napa Valley produce. Certainly a novice wine-maker will want to check out sources and prices in his own state (while tracking down a grape wholesaler in the nearest large city who handles wine grapes freighted in from California).

First-quality wine grapes are cultivated extensively in upstate New York and in Ohio. Maryland, too, produces superior wine grapes, though in smaller amounts. The same is true of New Jersey and Delaware. It is likely that small vineyards are nurtured wherever the climate is moderate, the rainfall sufficient, and the soil suitable for grape culture. Such small holdings are likely to have Italian or Swiss *patrons*, wine-makers

Wholesale Prices

themselves, who will sell at wholesale prices if you pick up at the vineyard. Some may permit or encourage you to harvest your own. Two problems arise here, although the experience of gathering grapes can be the happiest of family-and-friend outings.

Choose with Care

The first problem is simply that you may buy or harvest *fruit* grapes, such as Concords, Niagaras or Muscats, instead of true *wine* grapes. Before making a commitment to buy, go to a large supermarket and look at the fruit grapes for sale. Buy a small bunch of each variety and familiarize yourself with their tastes by eating them. Knowledge from nibbling. You *can* make palatable table wine from these three varieties. Full directions for doing so can be found by turning to the section HOME FRUIT WINES. However, wine from *wine* grapes is made from juice crushed and pressed from Zinfandel, Alicante, and Petit Syrah varieties, to name the most common. Zinfandels are the most widely grown, coast to coast. The home wine-maker may discover that his grape wholesaler carries or can order in bulk other wine grapes such as Cabernet Sauvignon or Pinot Noire reds and Pinot Chardonnay whites. These are premium wine grapes and fetch premium prices. The novice should wait a few seasons, strengthening his powers of anticipation, before he tries these. The methods laid forth here will assure a wine better than anybody else's while using the wine grapes most available to everybody. One of the secrets, as you will see, is in *blending* varieties.

Wine from Wine Grapes

Chester & Co.

For the past decade, the *La Mancha* wine-

makers have been buying grapes from wholesalers at a freight-siding located in the nearest
big city. The California varieties are shipped in
by train and trailer truck, arriving on or after
Columbus Day, roughly the second weekend in
October. The wholesalers buy in car-lots and sell

Your friendly grape wholesaler.

by the box. Sophisticates among them will take a
check (reluctantly) but prefer cash. The average.
dealer is a dollars-only type.

    Not all wholesale dealers are reputable. You
may expect to encounter fast-talking hustlers,
less aggressive ask-me-no-questions-I'll tell-you-
no-lies purveyors, and a fair percentage of gentlemen of Italian descent as honest as they are interested in having you buy from them year after

Caveat Emptor   year. An old acquaintance named Chester
vacillated between the first two categories. You
could buy from him, and we did, but it was strict-
ly a *caveat emptor* relationship.

When buying from a freight-yard whole-saler, get there early, bring the gang and perhaps a camera, and plan to stay until noon.

Whether you are in Brooklyn, Philadelphia, Boston or points west, you are making a good scene. Freight cars and truck trailers cover many acres, and by mid-morning the place is swarming with sellers, buyers, wives, kids, cousins, station wagons, dump trucks and pickups. Everyone is conversing at shout-level, lunging in and out of boxcars and trailers, tasting grapes, bargaining, rescuing kids from beneath truck wheels, closing deals, and counting the take. Wear your old clothes, not your snappiest Bermudas. Cruise from car to car, truck to truck. Find out who is selling what and what their price is per box. Sample liberally, but let your face be an impassive mask.

Correct Costume

What is a Good Grape?

While fruit grapes for the table are large, plump fruits in loose clusters, wine grapes are small and grow in clusters so tight they appear to be solid dark lumps. They are at their peak when their taste is so sweet as to be cloying. (Bring some dry bread along for a palate-cleansing between samples.) Wine grapes of good quality are *not terribly juicy*, at least at first handling or initial nibble. The skins are dark and thin, quite unlike the tough hide that shields the mollusklike Concord. A good Zinfandel or Alicante has soft flesh, surprisingly large seeds, and is really too sweet to eat with pleasure. You will notice finicky, tough-bargaining greyheads all about you munching two or three grapes. With eloquent frowns and grimaces of disgust, they spit out pulp and seeds, shrug, and wander away. Watch where they go.

How to Taste a Grape

The gestures and accusations in dialect are part of the whole bargaining ritual. They don't eat the grapes, because the too-sweet taste confuses the search. They may be back in twenty minutes with seven cousins and a diesel dump truck to bear away a couple of tons. Watch out for these oblique moves, and check prices. Normally, bargaining throughout the morning will cause the price per box to drop slightly, ten to fifteen cents, *seldom* as much as a quarter per box. No matter what you pay, the Chesters of the world will complain of near-bankruptcy while pocketing your cash. (Some of the most accomplished tragedians of the continent perform daily in big-city freight yards during the three-week period when grapes are sold.)

Ask and Bargain

It is best *not* to buy during the first weekend. Make the trip, get a few names and prices, and see what varieties are available. Ask questions. The Ali Babas of the boxcars will assure you that the best can be had that day only "in this car right over here." Shrug them off. Other dealers will say they have only Zinfandels this week but come back next Saturday for good Alicantes and Petit Syrrahs. Don't be stampeded. If prices hold steady, the choice *will* be greater the following weekend, most likely. Unless you are simply reckless, no one will cheat you in cold blood. It's a tough business, and the fruit is perishable. The dealers want a quick, large-volume sale, and you are a small-volume buyer out to get the best for your money.

How Much to Buy?

If you are buying from a vineyard, a second problem arises, and that is weight. Bushel baskets, especially those you pick yourself, will weigh less the longer you work. It is not laziness that urges you to declare the fifth bushel "full" with a clear two inches still to go, but rather impatience. Busheled grapes should be weighed on the vineyard's scales, for the general rule of thumb is: *fifteen pounds of grapes will make one gallon of wine.* If your goal is fifty gallons, you need 750 pounds.

15 lbs = 1 gal.

Wine grapes bought at a freight yard are sold by the box, in one of two weights: thirty-six pounds per box or, more common, forty-two pounds per box. Therefore, to make fifty gallons of wine, you will require from eighteen to twenty-one boxes. For larger amounts, double or triple your purchase. The need for helpers and station wagons should be clear at once. The boxes are bulky and require handling at least twice, loading and unloading. Small children can get crushed fingers and strained backs trying to help. Make your small-fry sub-Apprentices box-counters, not loaders. This is man's work, but not, of course, the Master Vintner's. The Master strikes the bargain and may choose to load the first box and the last. He pays the dealer and leaves his name, address, and phone number for next year. It is common for wholesale merchants to issue alluring postcards about a month before the freight yards fill. Grapes are your chosen avocation these days. Grapes have been the business of Chester and his cronies for several generations.

Manhandling

Drive home carefully. You are transporting several hundred pounds, and your wagon will steer poorly and brake much more slowly than normal. With a car full of kids, subordinate slaves, and grapes, you have a precious cargo indeed. Break neither springs nor speed records.

**Quantity vs.
Quality**

**"Zins" and
"Pets"**

You may be offered, or notice others buying, Muscat grapes, big, fat ones. Traditionally, these make lots of nice juice but indifferent to awful wine. Why bother? Buy Alicantes or Zinfandels and some Petit Syrrahs. Two-thirds of either Alicantes or "Zins" blended with one-third "Pets" will produce a deep ruby-colored wine of good bouquet and roast-beef-and-duckling dryness. Do not expect a Grand Cru burgundy or prize-winning bordeaux. You have not bought that kind of grape. You will have a superior dry, red American table wine that is *not* a Chianti and not "red ink." The Petit Syrrah grapes—small grapes, almost black; they resemble supermarket raisins and may, at peak, contain so much sugar that fructose crystals form within the pulp—these are the home wine-makers' treasures! So favored are the sugar-laden "Pets" that some heroes of the cellar blend their wine fifty-fifty. The glass, filled, is almost opaque, for the wine is a very dark purple. The taste is heavy, powerful, and pungent in after-flavor. The domestic quaff of gladiators, charioteers, and followers of Garibaldi. I can recall, dimly, splitting a bottle of one hundred percent pure Petit Syrrah wine. Somebody else drove home.

**The Secret is in
the Sugar**

Zinfandel and Alicante grapes alone produce abundant liquid for your needs, when purchased in the weight amounts indicated. These grapes contain enough sugar to make a rather light red, the color of a good beaujolais, about ten percent alcohol by volume. Although it improves by aging, it should be drunk young, finished by the end of the second year. There is simply not enough alcohol to insure good staying qualities.

The extra sugar of the Petit Syrrah grapes, however, raises the percentage of alcohol and guarantees a wine that will "round" nicely and will be better the second or third year. Wine made fifty-fifty with "Pets" can be stored until your grandchildren get baptized. Or married.

Saccha-rimetering

A saccharimeter is a handy, low-cost instrument useful to the novice, who is surrounded by Doubting Thomases of both sexes. Floated in a pickle jar of fresh-pressed juice, it will indicate the percentage of sugar. It should measure *at least* eighteen percent sugar content, for sugar-count is *twice* that of alcohol . . . in this case, nine percent. Safer is stronger, twenty percent and up. *A saccharimeter is an absolute necessity for all wines made from orchard fruits*, since all such juices need the addition of a sugar solution, even "sweet" cider.

Never apologize for making a blended wine. A large measure of the domestic wines of France are blends of "name-brand" grapes with their sturdy, darker brothers from Algeria. The Petit Syrrah, literally "small Syrian," is favored for its high sugar-count, high alcohol yield, as well as its rich flavor and solid coloring abilities.

Crushers and Crushing

The Master Vintner should have the crusher waiting in the cellar the day the grapes are bought. He may have bought one, rented or borrowed it. The crusher may be hand-powered by some Apprentice attached to the business end of the crank or driven by an electric motor. The electric ones work faster but are heavier to move about and more costly to rent or buy.

The slope-sided body of the crusher is designed to hold one full box of wine grapes. Pry off

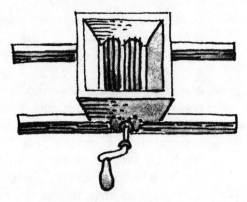

A hand-powered crusher.

the covers, squat, and heave up and over. Easy the first few times, until you get the hang of it. Opening the boxes and carting out the empties is Apprentice labor and the kind of job kids love.

An electric-powered crusher.

Loading the crusher is fair Journeyman's work, provided he is not receiving chiropractic attention. The Master supervises, perhaps tossing up and over the first box, taking a spin on the crusher crank, and seeing that the empties are swiftly removed. His prime function, however, is to see

Same for Each that *each fermenting barrel receives the same amount of the blended grapes.* He notes the day of crushing, orders a careful clean-up, and covers the barrels with several sheets of newspaper to discourage colonization of the crushed grapes by fruit flies.

Crushing is a cheerful, noisy affair that lasts long enough to give everyone a chance at all subtasks without becoming a bore. The grapes are really smashed, each one, with devil-may-care abandon. No point in picking out stems and vine leaves. Into the fermenters with the total contents of the boxes, including clusters dropped by accident. Alcohol is a great disinfectant. All stems, leaves, and trash will float to the top as the juice ferments. And a word here to Master Vint-

N. B. Yeasts ners with anxious wives: THE GRAPES ARE NOT TO BE WASHED! NEVER! The dull-dusty surface of each grape contains microscopic yeasts, those splendid little growths that activate, operate, and terminate the entire fermentation. A passion for cleanliness (no doubt a subconscious reaction to prolonged exposure to television commercials) must, at this point, be checked with utter firmness. To call a wine grape "dirty" is false! It is yeasted and ready to go. The robe of Mother Nature never needs bleach.

Boil and As soon as all grapes are thoroughly crushed,
Bubble clean and scrub the crusher with warm water and

a scrub brush. If owned, it may be left to dry before storage; if rented, it should be returned, pronto, to avoid paying more than one day's fee. Each fermenting barrel will contain a heady mash of stalks, pulp, juice, and the odd vine leaf with more pulp, it may seem, than juice. It will be very sweet to the taste and cool. Each fermenter should be about *two-thirds full*, no more. After the crowd departs, the Master Vintner should walk abroad in search of a *"chapeau* stick," a sturdy, green tree limb ending with two or three trimmed fingers. This is to stir the crushed grapes with. A two-by-

2/3 = Full

A chapeau *stick. (Barrels should be covered with several sheets of newspaper.)*

four with a small chunk nailed across one end will do as a substitute for an organic *chapeau* stick.

Nothing will happen for the first twenty-four hours. The cool, pulp-laden juice must warm before the natural yeasts begin to act on the crushed fruit-sugars. The second or third day, an ear pressed against the sides of the fermenting barrels will detect the faintest bubble and seethe. The *chapeau* will have formed—a thick topping of skins, stalks, leaves, and pulp pushed up by the early fermenting action.

Chapeau

The *chapeau* should be broken up and pressed down, stirred and plunged into the fermenting juice *twice daily*. When this is done, the juice will appear to "boil." It is highly effervescent, as bubbly as soda-pop, luke-warmish, and quite sweet. The Master may plunge and stir before leaving for the office in the morning and before dinner at night. He can swagger a bit. His grapes are about their business, and all's well with the world. If he is about *his* business, he will have arranged for a wine press, plastic buckets, and a large funnel, and given orders for all subordinates to stand by.

Fermentation

In the normal cellar, fermentation will take one week, from Saturday to Saturday. The *chapeau* will rise higher in the barrel each day and will change color to a rather flat, pale purple.

"Must"

Most of the pulp will have simply vanished, converted now to "must," the technical term for fermented grape juice. Some of the skins, too, will have dissolved; the remainder is soft and dull lilac in hue. During fourth and fifth day, the must will boil at a brisk burble-and-hiss, and froth will rush up from holes poked in the *chapeau* with the churning-stick.

On the sixth day following crushing, the action will slow. The *chapeau* when broken up, pushed down, and stirred will seem rather flimsy, with more "give" than before. That night, it will not push back up to its previous height. The boiling is nearly over, although the juice is still fermenting. You will notice a considerable amount of carbonation. Simply stated, fermentation is the process by which the yeasts convert sugar to alcohol; the carbon dioxide gas is a harmless by-product.

Fermentation Time

In really cool cellars, fermentation may last up to ten days. At temperatures above seventy-five degrees, the vigorous action may be completed in five. Hence the importance of the stick. The *chapeau* is the thing to watch, both for progressive weakness in consistency and for steady color change to that flat, unprepossessing pale purple. When the *chapeau* looks ready for the garbage pail, the must beneath is ready for the press.

The Master Vintner: A Study in Graduated Equality

From purchase through fermentation, opportunities abound for the novice vintner to seize and hold Master status. He should have negotiated for the grapes, arranged for unloading, demonstrated the brawny but brief techniques of crushing, and accepted all the "Gee, it's-easier-than-I-thought!" comments from family and underlings with the half-shrugs and quizzical muted smiles that convey A Great Mind At Work. Build on this drama. Let Journeymen brag and Apprentices babble.

The Master at "Work"

The sight of the Master inclined in silent scrutiny over a bubbling barrel will reduce them to puzzlement and awe. They have been fooled. The thing is much more complex than they thought. Ruination and fifty gallons of vinegar lie ahead, enough to toss in their salads for six disappointing decades! (The Master creates anxiety, while feeling none himself.)

Witnesses may observe him plunge and churn with forked stick or two-by-four. They are sure to ask, "How's it coming?" The obvious reply, "Fine!", is obviously incorrect. The Master should mutter: "The *chapeau* is appropriately stiff. As expected," or "Yes, exactly. The must is working." Under no circumstance should the Master translate these jargon-terms. The mystery of his utterances is both means and ends. For the Master, the innocence of others is his greatest strength. His strange words, combined with an aura of *absolute confidence,* will imply a control of natural forces just slightly short of wizardry. He may take these days of secret chemistry to display an openness, a generosity towards his underlings. Journeyman and Apprentices will not see such kindness again until the last cork is driven into the final bottle. The Master is very wise, they will think. He has knowledge beyond our grasp. Our best hope is to obey, to serve him blindly. He is the brain, we but the willing hands.

The P of GE

By the time the press has been bought, borrowed or rented, the Principle of Graduated Equality should have been fixed firmly in the weak heads of all underlings. They are the same as the Master. He is one of them. They will demonstrate their equalness by doing *exactly* what he tells them to do, the *instant* he gives an order. Since he obviously cannot work and think at the same time, only an ingrate or insurrectionist would risk the wine by even the faintest challenge to his mystique-shrouded authority. His wife prepares his favorite dinner dishes. Unruly off-spring walk on tip-toes in his presence. He summons his Journeyman and Apprentices. They cluster before him, gnawing their lips. The Master whips the faded sports section from the top of a fermenting barrel and points, once, to what lies within.

His Master's Voice

"We will press this, beginning at nine o'clock tomorrow. Be here on time!"

Note the egalitarian "we," bespeaking communal labor, fraternal toil for the good of all. Note, too, the final command, devoid of the namby-pamby "please," that cancels all golf games, dentist appointments, and trips to the car-wash. The Master has spoken.

THE TRADE OF TRICKS

Basket, Pins and Plate

A wine press is an intriguing object, engineered for its function alone, and devoid of beauty despite the deplorable habit of decorators who convert the smaller models to table lamps. Solid oak uprights support a low-rimmed box on a cross-member. The low box has a hole, perhaps lipped, through which the juice runs out into a bucket placed below. In the box sits the "basket," a cylinder of oak slats, open at both ends, held rigid by encircling steel hoops. The basket is hinged vertically, and when the retaining pins are lifted free of their slots, the whole affair opens easily. A flat wooden disc, usually reinforced, fits inside the basket, with a clearance of no more than one-eighth of an inch. This is the "plate." The reinforced side goes up to accept the pressure exerted by the impressive screw-shaft. The threaded shaft is lowered and raised by turning a knobbed handle at the top. The affair generates considerable force when run by a hefty Journeyman. It runs on the principle of "mechanical advantage" which few high school physics students ever encounter in real life. A wine press is really an upside-down jack designed to compress fermented grape pulp beneath the plate. The

Pressing—the La Mancha Method.

basket restrains the pressures sideways, and the box holds the juices and lets them run off to be collected and transferred to the aging barrel.

"Due to a Pressing Engagement..."

If crushing is a brief and brawny business, pressing is slow; an all-day affair, including the inevitable clean-up. Not only is it slow and sloppy work, but it is replete with seepy purple joys. Any male who likes to dig clams on a mud-flat or change the oil in his car will make an ideal wine-presser. Kids love it, for the first hour or so, until they realize that the process, interesting once, is to be repeated without variation until the fermenting barrels are empty and the aging casks full.

**Wine and
Women,
Again**

Women of any age find it simply the sort of messing around that males inexplicably adore. They will come down into the cellar, watch for a while, scatter a few newspapers about, and demand to know when the Master intends to release his happy wine-stained drudges for lunch. The average comment, "Well, I sure hope you plan to clean up all this mess! I've got the laundry to do down here!" should be quietly ignored. The Master replying, "Yes, dear," can only weaken a position hard-won by guile. He may grunt, flap his apron, and reply, *"Bene, bene."* But no more. "We" are busy.

**The Imperial
Pronoun**

Though pressing should never be rushed, the size or capacity of the press will affect the speed of the work. A small fruit press with a rigid basket holding no more than a pailful of pulp is a nuisance. Ideally, the basket should be large enough to take about half the contents of a fermenting barrel at one time. The hinges make the basket easier to empty. Time is best spent in the pressing itself, not the tedious task of unloading for the next batch. Get a press that is big enough. (They are bulky and heavy to horse down into a cellar and out again. Normally, setting up the press and cleaning it when done is the work of the Journeyman, assisted by at least one strong Apprentice).

Be Prepared

Again, and always, equipment should be brought to the cellar and kept handy. The entire floor area should be covered with old newspaper to catch spills. Optimum equipment for pressing:

One press.

Three two-gallon plastic pails, not the flimsy

Beyond the Pail

kind with handles that pull loose, but solid, sturdy, and not too flexible.

Two large kitchen strainers.

One big metal funnel, ideally the kind with a sieve at the base of the flare, used to process any kind of seeded juice.

Two lengths of two-by-four.

Scrub brush and baking soda (for cleaning the empty fermenters and the press).

Two empty grape boxes.

The La Mancha Method

Place a two-by-four beneath the rear legs of the press to tilt it. The must will run quickly from the box into the bucket set beneath the drip-hole. Set the funnel in the bung-hole of the opened aging barrel. (This barrel has been sulphured immediately after purchase, soaked to absolute tightness, flushed, emptied, sulphured again with half a stick, and bunged shut. The Journeyman is responsible for barrels, with the Master handling the brimstone and checking him at every step.

The Womb of Wine

This barrel is the womb of wine and must be in perfect health to produce delightful off-spring year after year.) The bung-hole should be upright, of course.

Press the second plastic bucket carefully down into the *chapeau* of the first fermenter. The juice will be abundant and will spill into the bucket, sweeping along in its flood odd stalks, leaf skeletons, and the residue of grape skins. When about two-thirds full, lift it free, carry it to the funnel, and wait until an Apprentice has set one of the large strainers inside the funnel. Pour the must carefully into the barrel. The strainer will catch the heavier debris, much of which will be seeds. Knock this junk out into the second empty grape box.

"Baling" a Barrel

Repeat this process with unhurried care. This is called "baling." About two-thirds of the contents of the fermenting barrels is liquid. As much as possible should be simply strained into the aging barrel. There is no need to press that which is already fluid. Baling displaces the sulphur gas in the aging barrel as each bucket is added. Hold your breath as you pour as the odor is powerful and choking. Don't worry. There is not a great deal of gas, and it diffuses easily and harmlessly into the air. The coming-and-going of workers and visitors during pressing will ensure safe ventilation.

After five or six buckets have been baled, the pulp will overflow into the pushed-down buckets to such a degree that when emptied, the contents will clog and flood over the strainer. Anticipate this and shift to the press before spilling your treasure.

Pouring Pulp

The basket should be open, but securely locked with its retaining pins. The screw should be raised all the way up, the plate set aside within easy reach. Pour and paw the sloppy, rich-fumed pulp and liquid into the basket. Dark juice will rush through the basket-sides to be caught in the container set below. Fill the basket to the top and press the pulpy mass down gently and evenly, so the plate will lie flat when set on top. Even a half-hearted push should send juice gushing through the basket-slats. As soon as the container below becomes more than half-full, slide an empty in place and pour the juice through the strainer and funnel into the aging barrel. Place the plate so that it does not bind against the inside of the basket and spin down the screw.

Easy does it! Take a few turns. Rest a minute. Another few turns. The pulp is sodden, and the buckets beneath the press will fill rapidly at first.

Soon the unappetizing mass in the basket will release less, and the wheel will become hard to turn. Most press-wheels have two metal knobs on the top. Slide your second two-by-four between them, making a handle. Suddenly, what resisted, yields. You swing one end of the plank, and your force is increased by the length of the simple lever you have made. Obviously, this should be demonstrated by the Master, but as a throw-away. Such clever use of simple physical laws may not occur to your brawny but dim-witted Apprentices, but once they are shown, they seldom forget. Just make certain they recall *from whom they learned.*

Handling the Press

One revolution and rest. The juices trickle now, no longer an impetuous gush. Certainly all the kids about will have tasted the juice. Adults will lick their fingers and mutter accusingly, "Doesn't taste much like wine to me!" The Master laughs softly, shaking his head at such innocence. He should discourage his crew from actually drinking what is still, technically, must, for the fermentation is not yet completed. Imbibed in bulk, this sweet but rather murky beverage will taste sweet, slightly bubbly; not too bad, in fact, but not wine, to be sure. Once it hits the human stomach, it ferments a second time, with a vengeance. Must is a powerful diuretic, as well as intoxicating. It will scour the unwary Apprentice from duodenum to lower tract and leave him weary, weak, and wary. Taste, yes. Drink, no!

Drive the plate down hard. From filling the basket to the Master's command to unload ("Break out the cake!") consumes at least *thirty minutes* of deliberate, paced, squeeze-and-rest, with buckets emptied slowly but steadily through the strainer and funnel into the barrel. The screw now cannot be turned. The juice dribbles and stops. Apprentices stand puzzled. "What cake?"

How Fast is Good?

The Master sighs, sets hand to timber, and spins up the screw. He lifts the plate free, exposing a broad, flat plug of pulp rammed solid by the pressure. A gesture brings the Journeyman to help. They lift the basket free, out of the box, and set it on top of an empty grape crate. The Master pulls the retaining pins from the locks on the side of the basket, opens the basket, and gives it a slight shake. Hey, *presto!* With an impressive, seed-scattering thud, a cake of skins, stalks, seeds, and purple bits drops into the crate. It looks like a plug of chewing tobacco for a giant. The cake is damp to the touch and compressed so solid that it can be broken into lumps only with a hatchet. The Master hands the retaining pins to the Journeyman, then points from the basket to the press. He has worked his magic again. Surely if under his direction solids can be formed from soggy pulp, great wine will be produced from this purplish fluid poured into the aging cask. Press on!

The "Cake"

Repeat all steps as above. Bale first, then pour the pulp into the press until the basket is full. Work the plate down slowly, squeezing out every precious drop. Lift the basket out, free the cake, and have some Apprentice lug it up to the back lawn. The cake makes superior garden mulch. Since the grapes' seeds have been swirled about in fermenting, the alcohol produced prevents them from sprouting. They will never germinate into a backyard vineyard, more's the pity.

Topping-Off

Scraping the bottom of the fermenting barrels to get the last bits is a heady experience. The fumes of alcohol are strong enough to make the eyes of the toughest Apprentice water. In big professional vineyards, the huge oak tuns are cleaned by workers wearing oxygen masks, for the fermenting process consumes the oxygen entirely. Like the sulphur fumes, the gas remaining in the bottom of the fermenters should *not* be breathed. You won't get sick, but you *may* well feel woozy. And nobody loves a woozy Apprentice.

An All-Purpose Response

After several hours' labor, each half pail added seems as though it must certainly overflow the aging barrel. How *can* it hold more? Even when the liquid level has risen so that a finger thrust in the bung-hole comes away wet to the first knuckle, the barrel may still take three to five gallons. Finally, juice gushes around the funnel throat and overflows. The Journeyman curses those equals graded beneath him as bungling incompetents. Worse, now, it seems there is juice left over. Somewhere between one gallon and five. The Master nods. "For topping-off," he comments. "Oh," the Journeyman says. "Yeah."

The must gurgles gently at the bung-hole. Minute bubbles bead on the surface and break. Somehow it smells much more *winey!* The Master spreads a sheet of paper over the bung-hole and waves his subordinates on to their clean-up chores. The press must be dismantled, carried outside, and scrubbed under the house. The fermenting barrels must be flushed and scrubbed, once, twice, until every seed has been dislodged from each crevice, with much care given to in-

Clean-Up Time spections of the lower seam. The newspapers, soaked and trodden to wet fragments, must be picked up, the cellar floor washed and scrubbed. All strainers, sieves, and plastic buckets are rigorously cleaned, too. The cellar crew is soaked, tired, and triumphant. They are stained a dark red to the elbows. Their dungarees, covered with stains that can never be removed, will henceforth be identified as "my wine-making pants."

The last five gallons of wine have been strained into jugs or bottles. The aging barrel, to the alarm of many, remains open for forty-eight hours. When wood and wine wed, the former absorbs several quarts. The level in the barrel drops. The Master "tops off" from his jugs, once after the first day, again after the second. Yet another secret: the necessity of surplus.

Water-Seals Once the must is poured through strainers into the aging barrel, two processes begin. One process is the slow completion of fermentation. The second is "fining." In order to allow for total fermentation, you will need to buy or make one water-seal per aging barrel.

An intriguing and effective water-seal is available through merchants catering to the wine-making trade. It is a twisted tube of bent glass with a bulbous part filled with water, hence the name. Bore a hole in a wooden bung large enough to take the tube. Press or tap the bung in place.

Melt enough paraffin or common candle wax in a clean tin can to smear around the base of the glass tube and to cover the narrow crevice between the bung and the barrel itself.

A commercial water-seal.

Oxygen is the Enemy

The bulb part of the tube should be filled with water. Escaping carbon dioxide gas, even at very low pressure, can pass through water, but air cannot reach the wine. Once the must is in the aging barrel, the wine-maker's enemy is oxygen. Topping-off prevents an air space; the water-seal prevents air leakage. Oxygen will permit bacteria and mold to live and flourish. Given a chance, these invisible organisms will change what you have to a rather inferior vinegar. This must *never* happen!

An inexpensive water-seal can be made by using a ten-inch piece of quarter-inch plastic tubing or rubber hose fitted snug in a bored bung, with the open end *constantly* submerged in water. Poke a hole in a clean jar, fill it with water, and plunge the end of the tube deep. Make certain the water does not evaporate, allowing air to leak back into the barrel.

How Long under Water

Keep the aging barrel under water-seal for *one month.* Nothing dangerous or dramatic will

A homemade water-seal.

happen, if the Master sees to it that the seal, of either sort, has enough water. Gas seepage is so slow that you are not likely to see bubbles. Carbon dioxide is very soluble and passes in minute amounts into the water, floats to the surface, and vanishes like last month's pay check.

Bunging

After thirty days, carefully remove the water-seal on the aging barrel, first scraping away the wax from around the bung. Save this entire unit for all the years to come. You will note that the level in the barrel has again dropped. The barrel has absorbed more and perhaps as much as a gallon of gas has escaped safely, unnoticed. Top-off the barrel with excess wine. (All excess wine

Excess Wine

should be sealed carefully in gallon or half-gallon jugs or quart bottles with screw-on caps. Keep these bottle *filled,* and change to smaller measures as this surplus is used. The less surface of the wine exposed to air the better. Sniff and sip before topping-off. Do not add any surplus that smells "foxy" or tastes like vinegar. Fanaticism is not necessary, but precaution is.) The barrel should be filled *just below* the bottom of the bung-hole. Drive a fresh bung home firmly and plaster it with wax, making a *perfect* seal. This done, you have nothing to do but wait for one hundred days. Certainly this is ample time for a Wine-Maker's Lunch.

**La Mancha
Wine-Makers'
Lunch**

Apprentice Antipasto

Shred several types of lettuces—Iceberg, Romaine, Salad Bowl or Oak Leaf—to form a thick blanket covering a very large platter. Arrange, in tasteful and eye-pleasing patterns, thin-sliced hard salami, *prosciutto*, hard-boiled eggs, halved and sprinkled with paprika, some anchovies, one jar (at least) of artichoke hearts, a fist of slender green and white scallions, olives of several varieties (ripes, greens, and Greeks), chunky tomato wedges in plenty, thin golden sheaves of Swiss cheese and the white, whey lumps of Greek *Feta* cheese, that salty variety made of goats' milk, perhaps some radishes, frilled and soaked in water overnight to make them look like the roses they cannot taste like, and, always, several tins of first-class sardines, with their own accompanying lemon wedges. Yes!

Sprinkle over all these delicacies a palate-perking dressing of pure olive oil and wine vinegar (naturally), a dash of pepper and more of salt, beaten with a whisk or shaken to a perfect red-gold emulsion. Serve the antipasto lavishly on large dinner plates with plenty of French or Italian bread. *La Mancha* vintners and other *savants* prefer:

Posie's Pita (Near-Eastern Flat Bread)

Dissolve one envelope of yeast in slightly more than one cup of warm water. Use a large bowl and add three cups flour and two and a half teaspoons salt. The mixture, well stirred, will make a firm, gluey ball. Turn this lump out onto a floured bread board and knead it until it is satin smooth. (You may have to add a bit more flour.) Divide this lump into six small balls. Squeeze, hammer, and knead until each is smooth, glossy, and a perfect sphere. Take a rolling pin, re-dust the board with flour, and flatten the six balls until they are a quarter inch thick. They should be about five inches in diameter. Remove to a floured surface, a shelf or counter, cover with a flour-dusted dish towel, and allow to rise for forty-five minutes or more. Put the slightly puffed rounds on a greased baking sheet, and slide into a *very hot oven* (500 F.) for fifteen minutes. If you have a glass-doored oven, watch these little mothers puff until they look like tiny flying saucers. *Do not overbake!*

Just before serving, re-heat. The bread rounds will brown lightly, but the upper and lower layers will be separate. Cut them in half. They make perfect pockets to stuff with a crunchy, juicy serving of antipasto.

Pasta with Pesto

For a simple, substantial but sensational, or sensuous, main course, try this. *Warning:* You *must* have *fresh* leaves. If the front comes before October, gather your spinach or basil earlier, pack in freezer bags and hold until ready. Otherwise, gather enough basil leaves (or twelve to fifteen large spinach leaves) to jam-pack a one-cup measure to overflowing. Really pack them *solid*. Dump the compressed leaves into a blender with one cup grated Parmesan cheese and two-thirds of a cup of your best olive oil. Whir for thirty seconds. Add half a cup *each* parsley and blanched almonds (or pine nuts) and two teaspoons of salt. Whir for thirty seconds. Now, count heads at the table. Add two large cloves of garlic per person and one for the pot. Let the blender spin until you have a thick, bright-green, pungent, semi-solid sauce. *Slowly* add about one tablespoon of olive oil, blending again. The *pesto* should just barely pour, with the help of a spoon. This will serve six people or four gluttons. Keep the *pesto* at room temperature. Do *not* heat.

Boil thin spaghetti or number ten vermicelli *al dente* (firm). Drain and place in a large bowl. Add the *pesto,* one dollop at a time, tossing until each strand is splendidly coated. Serve.

Devour all this with generous amounts of Brand X red wine, which yours will surpass. Add French, Italian, or Greek folk music, wives, and cherished females. For dessert, just chilled fresh fruit and *espresso* coffee. *Bene, Bene!*

RACK OR RUIN

There is, alas, a good deal of wine made in cellars across the land that is indifferent-to-poor in quality. Thin, sour, cheek-puckery slosh. You have prevented this by careful purchase of Petit Syrrah grapes, blended with the others of your choice. Your wine will be as dark as Homer's sea, full-bodied with a rich bouquet . . . if you rack it twice. That is why you have a second aging barrel. For much wine that *could* be good is spoiled by omitting this important step.

"Racking" consists of pouring what has now become young wine into a clean barrel. With any sort of simple pump, the job does not take long, but, again, certain precautions must be observed.

Time to Rack
When the Master has checked off eighty days on his calendar, he instructs the Journeyman to prepare the second barrel (sulphured on the day of purchase like the one already containing the liquid treasure). The racking barrel should be filled with water until soaked leakproof, the water changed once. Since the months have rolled on from October to late December, an inexpensive

heater may be required to keep the water from freezing if the soaking is done outdoors. A simpler method is to bring the barrel down in the cellar, set it on its concrete block and timber rack beside the first and fill it with a hose. It should not leak much. The water can be pumped out the day before racking. *This barrel should be sulphured again, lightly, half a stick, two days before use.*

Siphons and Pumps

The Master will open the filled aging barrel after scraping the wax away from the bung. He will siphon off a glass and hold it to a strong light. It should be absolutely clear. He should inhale the bouquet and conceal his disappointment. Cool red wine has little real odor, although the Master can coax up a bit by warming the glass in his hands, while Apprentices whimper. The

Elementary Tasting

Master tastes, *makes no comment,* and passes the glass to the Journeyman. The Journeyman, sensitized by now to the cellar's system of Graduated Equality, knows he is permitted to comment, *if he dares.* He may sip and pass, earning points for diplomacy. He may finish the glass and say, "Yeaaah!" The latter is more common. By this time, the Apprentices are drooling, their empty hands outstretched. Since they are equals, the Master pours them a measure. The Apprentices crow and thump each other's shoulders and carry on generally. For the wine is *good,* there can be no question of that. It is *good* wine! The Master nods, slightly. Of course. *It is supposed to be good!*

Before the barrel is plundered and congratulations turn to excessive mirth and song, the Master recovers the communal glass and gives orders for the pump or siphon to be set up. In

**Racking
Equipment**

either case, he must have the following equipment handy:

>One wooden quarter-inch dowel, four feet long.
>One ball of fine string.
>Clear plastic tubing, softened and flexible from a soak in warm water.
>One large funnel, presumably the one used in pressing processes.
>One strainer, also previously used in pressing.
>One package of cheesecloth, sometimes called "jelly cloth," the sturdy gauze that makes an admirable and cheap filter.

The Journeyman opens the racking barrel. The Master carefully lowers the dowel down into the wine and gently lifts it straight up. He marks the mid-point of the wine-stained part of the dowel by tying the string at the point, leaving ends to hang free (the string should be long enough to tie the plastic tubing to the dowel at

Tubing and racking.

that point). The Master notes with great care the lower end of the dowel. It is coated with a thin, lilac film, unpleasant to the touch, sight, and taste. The dowel tip may be so coated for a good

The "Lees"

two inches, ideally less, and often a bit more. This pale-purple sludge is the "lees." The purpose of racking is to siphon or pump off the clear wine so that the lees may be discarded. The curve of the wine barrel is designed to catch and hold the lees. Since this is so, the barrel must not be tilted, tipped, or rolled about during racking. The wine itself should be agitated as little as possible.

The plastic tubing should be tied in three or four places to hold it along the dowel. Though the tubing is now affixed to the mid-point of the dowel, it must be long enough to eventually reach from just above the lees to the cellar floor (if a conventional siphon is to be used) without kinking, or from just above the lees to the bung-hole of the racking barrel if a pump is to be employed.

Siphoning

La Mancha wines have been siphoned for over a decade, to the delight of Apprentices. Once the tube is fastened snugly to the dowel, an Apprentice is applied to the loose end. He sucks briskly, creating suction, swallows the delightful dividend, and drops the tube into a waiting plastic pail. The wine purls through the tubing and the bucket fills. When half full, it is carried to the racking barrel. A single layer of cheesecloth lines the funnel. The wine is poured into the racking barrel. Since the wine will run non-stop until the vacuum created is broken (when the barrel is half-emptied), all Apprentices must be nimble and see that no bucket overflows. The cheesecloth filter should be changed every three or four buckets. The gauze will pick up a certain amount of goop, actually pulverized grape skins held in suspension, indicating it is doing its job.

When the suction is broken at the half-way point, the Master slides the tube down the dowel, half-way between the top of the lees and the previous point. A fresh Apprentice is applied to the tube and the siphon-fill-empty cycle is repeated until the suction is broken again.

Quality Control

Of course, quality control must be maintained. It is traditional for the Master to fill the glass at fairly regular intervals for color, bouquet, and taste testing. The Journeyman, refreshed and stimulated by these periodic product samplings, exudes benevolence to the point of addressing the Apprentices by their given names. Morale, generally, rises as the level of the wine sinks. Banter and song are not uncommon. Wives and cherished women are invited to "have a taste." Children clamor for a sip. And the first pailful is spilled by some Apprentice too long at the tube.

While siphoning has its very real delights, it

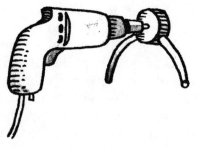

An electric pump.

cannot be denied that is it slow work. Often a certain recklessness is noted, even at the Journeyman level of labor. For this reason, *La Mancha* workers invested, reluctantly, in a simple rotary

Pumping

pump that attaches to a quarter-inch electric drill. The free end of the tube is fitted snugly to one end of the pump (which is some three inches in diameter and half an inch thick, really very small) and another, shorter section to the other end of the pump, running into the racking barrel. Once set up, the Master starts the drill, and the wine is pumped from barrel to barrel in jig-time. The tube is slipped down the dowel until all the wine is drawn off the lees.

Clear Plastic Tubing

The last inch or so is crucial, for the suction of either siphon or pump will begin to lift the lees. The tube must be clear plastic so the first appearance of murkier wine can be observed. Even though murky, this wine can be carefully filtered into the racking barrel. But *not* anything that shows as opaque or tinged violet.

Save the Dregs!

It always seems a shame and a waste to discard the last inch or so. This need not be. If the Master has taken the caution to provide a number of gallon and half-gallon jugs with clean screw caps and an odd quart bottle or two with tight closures, this wine can be tapped from the aging barrel and simply set aside. It will fine itself; that is, each bottle will reproduce in miniature the slow settling of the lees to the bottom. It will never be the best produced in a given year, but is perfectly suitable for topping-off the barrel during the second racking. Carefully siphoned and filtered, it can be blended with the rest at bottling time.

One-Barrel Vintners vs. The Monastic School

It is possible, obviously, to rack your wine into sufficient gallon jugs, large containers, or ten-gallon glass carboys, and then drag the barrel outside, flush the lees out with care and pour

**Carboy
Storage**

the wine back in the *original* aging barrel. There are certainly too many containers to get dropped, kicked over or otherwise wasted. It is accepted practice, but less efficient than the Monastic School, or two-barrel racking. Two barrels linked by our simple drill-powered pump has reduced *La Mancha* man-hours and spillage-loss so markedly that no other system is likely to be employed in the vintage years that lie ahead. Use of the second barrel allows the first to "breathe," and since it must be soaked and sulphured before the mid-April *second* racking, the vintners are protected from the dread bacteria. If his only barrel has gone bad, the one-barrel vintner is in real trouble.

**Water-Seal and
Bung Again**

The racking barrel must be topped-off as before, water-sealed as before (for the wine has been stirred up by the siphon or pump), the seal removed and a bung meticulously sealed in place.

**Second
Racking**

Rack in early January and again in April. The *second* racking will show less than an inch of lees on the dowel tip, if you have all worked well. The wine will have lightened in color toward a deep burgundy hue. A mild, still-fruity bouquet is more easily released by warm hands. The wine tastes less "rough." It is, as they say, just beginning to "round."

A happy phrase, one both optimistic and obscure. No Journeyman or Apprentice can be certain that a round wine is preferred or even desirable until the Master utters the word, smacking his lips and smiling slightly. (At the wine, not at the incompetents who labor at his direction and whim.) But, remembering that they are only human and graded in equality so long as they serve him, he sets the water-seal, marks off thirty days again on his calendar, discards his apron and green eye-visor and waves his serfs upstairs for A Bung-Bangers' Brunch. He follows their happy ascent, carrying with him one bottle he has siphoned off and set aside. Oh, it is not really *ready*, yet. Bottling will not take place until May. But still, it might be a pleasant little experiment to see just how well "our wine" stacks up against Brand X. The women will be pleased, the underlings flattered. The Master is not parched to agony. He is, simply, curious and rather proud. He just wants "to see." The Master, too, is only human.

When to Bottle

A Bung-Bangers' Brunch

Efficient racking of one barrel begun on the dot of 8:30 will be completed, with barrels flushed clean and cellar floor scrubbed, well before noon, barring mishaps. Since racking is a mid-winter and raw early-spring business, substantial viands are called for, succulent stews prepared with or flavored with wine, something French or authentically Greek. Something like:

Greek Spinach and Scallion Pie

This single-dish brunch for second-racking is robust enough to go it alone, supported by Syrian bread, a simple dessert, and red wine in brimming bumpers.

Chop two bunches of scallions, washed and trimmed of root hairs. Use the crisp white heads and pungent green tails. Sauté in two tablespoons of butter until tender, remove from the heat and set aside.

Chop two pounds of washed and drained spinach and place in a large pan, cover tightly and cook until wilted. Drain, pressing out as much liquid as possible, toss about to loosen, and press again. Pour the cooked scallions and buttery juices into the spinach.

Make two pie crusts, either from your own favorite recipe or from prepared mixes. Roll out thin. You should have enough to line a one-and-a-half quart casserole dish, with enough left over to make the top crust. Butter your dish, lower your liner into place, pat and poke until you work the lower crust up to the rim of the dish. Toast the lined dish in a 350 degree oven for five to ten minutes, just enough to make sure it won't go soggy on you. Remove from the oven.

Add to your pot of cooked scallions and spinach half a pound of crumbled *Feta* cheese, half a pound thick curd cottage cheese, and one cup chopped parsley. Salt and pepper liberally and mix well. Beat six whole eggs with one tablespoon of flour until well blended, but not frothy. Add this to your pot of goodnesses and mix around again. Pour it all into your lined casserole dish. Make your top crust secure over all, pinching it firmly around the rim. Cut out a round hole the size of a quarter and discard the disc of dough. Brush the top crust with melted butter. Put the dish on a cookie sheet. Bake for about an hour, perhaps an hour and a quarter. Brush once in cooking with melted butter. It will smell delicious, and be a golden brown when done. Remove from the oven and let stand for ten minutes or about halfway through one side of a record of Greek folk music and half-way through the first bottle of red. Serve cut into plump, juicy wedges.

Experiment with herbs here, a teaspoon of oregano or a half a cup of *fresh* dill, or a quarter cup bruised and minced basil leaves. Be bold,

Zorba and Melina

for this dish is styled to satisfy five famished Zorbas and their consorts. Be prepared for dancing and mirth.

Brew a bucket of Greek or Turkish coffee, powerful and black as a mortgage-holder's heart. Sweeten with honey. A final flourish here is *ouzo,* a Greek liqueur, poured over crushed ice. A shrewd Master will have seen his cellar cleaned *before* these festivities of cup and fork begin. An Apprentice full of spinach-and-scallion pie, red wine, and *ouzo* is not a man who can be ordered below stairs to scrub a floor. Not at all. He is out in the kitchen dancing with a lady who is *not* his wife. (This combination tends to bring out the Melina Mercouri in them all.) Perhaps a long, cooling walk will be in order.

Beef and Beans

A less volatile dish, but rich and revitalizing. Should be prepared the day before and reheated for serving.

Cut half a pound of bacon into squares, separate the slices and brown in a deep kettle. Remove the bacon to drain on paper towels. Cut two pounds of good stew beef into cubes, *dry thoroughly,* dust with pepper and brown on all sides in the bacon fat. Remove the meat to a dish, temporarily.

Figure one onion per person, with an extra one for the Master. Peel and chop coarsely, sauté in the bacon fat until soft and golden. Remove the sautéed onions and place with the beef. Stare thoughtfully at the remaining bacon fat. Consider that how much you let remain will determine the richness of the dish. Many do not care for the heavy, unctuous savor of bacon ren-

Esquimaux and Whalers

derings. Those possessed of Esquimaux blood or lineal descendents of Nantucket whalers will have this dish in full glory. Remove the liquid fat and leave the amount you feel suitable or wise. Allow this to cool, so that when you replace the beef and onions, these ingredients will not sauté a second time.

Purists will insist on half a can of tomato paste, untouched and undiluted, stirred in. This is proper measure if you have gone heavy on the bacon fat for you are balancing oil with acid. If prudence has dictated a limited use of bacon fat, add one tablespoon of tomato paste and half a cup of ketchup. Finicky souls may stick to one cup of ketchup and ignore the tomato paste. Stir about what you have added.

Pour over all enough red wine to cover the meat. Now simmer until the beef is tender.

Cautious types will cool the contents of the kettle, skim off the fat on the surface and discard it. Gourmands will shrug contemptuously and add enough cloves of crushed garlic to de-kink the Master's mustache. When cooled, you may place the kettle in any refrigerator big enough to hold it. A simpler method is just to let it rest. The ingredients will "get married," as the saying goes. Out of opposites, you make one sauce, pungent and savory. What you add will improve what you have made, an elevation, nay, an apotheosis!

Count the gluttons gathered in the cellar. Put the kettle on to warm, *gently.* Add at least one fifteen-ounce can of red kidney beans, the big plump ones, undrained, for the Master and two cans (of this same size) for every three subordinates. If you think big, just add two huge cans. Warm slowly, mixing the beef-onions-and-sauce in with the kidney beans. ONLY KIDNEY BEANS! Any other variety is too soft, too mushy.

Chop an entire bunch of parsley, at least two cups. Sprinkle all this bright green freshness on the surface of the piping hot stew, just before you bear the whole kettle to the table. Ladle into deep bowls and pass around hot, crusty bread to sop up the sauce. The second bowlful will set the bung-bangers to pounding on the table and pledging your name with refilled glasses.

Calories Don't Count

This dish deserves the attention of your taste buds to get the balance of flavors you prefer. Adjust it as you will. You really can't go wrong. Remember, it is *supposed* to be rich, thick, pungent, and fattening. The meat is tender, but still firm, the blandness of the kidney beans braced with the tang of garlic and tomato. The ingredients are common stuff, but their marriage is a joy and a satisfaction.

Take care not to over-frill this kind of brunch. No little appetizer nibbles of inflated cheese-dust, pressed chaff and preservatives. No elaborate desserts dredged in goo. Serve a single dish to feed the appetites whetted by racking (and tasting) the wine. Simple, strong, solid food, unadorned. Full glasses and filled bellies, smiles and songs. Another bottle once around? Well, a drop . . . all right, half a glass, then. A toast!

A Toast for Masters

"My comrades of the cellar, our labors well-begun have aged and mellowed into wine of great promise, although it is still, like you, my brothers of bung and barrel, young and strong! My heart lifts to see you at this table, your comely women at your sides. You are witty, and she is gay. You have each chosen well, for I find that you make a *most attractive* couple! Your sons are sturdy-limbed and full of promise, nimble with crates and buckets. Your daughters are clear of eye, sweet-fleshed, and kissable. Surely they will marry for love, both well and wisely, and the fruit of these tender vines shall be the full fresh promise of our vintage years. Companions of cask and cheesecloth, good stewards of siphons and sieves, I salute you! We have crushed and pressed and racked, and now the future spreads wide before us—broad vistas of snowy linen, flowers in loose bloom, and crystal glasses that hold scents and savors and songs that we have caught together in the ruby beauty of our wine. I drink to Master, Journeymen and Apprentices all! You are the best of fellows, my comrades, at work and at this table over plate and glass. I am grateful to you all, for it is through you that I know that I am happy, that God is kind, that men and women love and that life is very, very sweet!"

From left to right: Claret, Burgundy and Champagne bottles.

BEAUTIFUL, BEAUTIFUL BOTTLES

About thirty days after the second racking, the Master will give the long-awaited command: "We will bottle this weekend." The Apprentices go half-mad with joy. Dogs bark, maidens weep, bells ring, and prisoners are set free. The Journeyman shrugs and smiles indulgently. Bottles are really little of his affairs. He is a barrel-man, after all, used to thinking big. Because of this, he must be watched. Journeymen are inclined to measure by the gallon and to have their wine in jumbo measures. The Master, however, sees wine by the fifth bottle, corked and waxed, snugly binned against the long months ahead.

Kinds of Bottles

Wine bottles come in three traditional shapes: Claret, Burgundy, and Champagne. Normally, each contains one-fifth of a gallon. Five per gallon times fifty in the aging barrel equals 250 bottles, less spills, shrinkage, and sips. It goes without saying, I hope, that nobody ever buys an *empty* wine bottle. Full ones, yes, that are emptied, rinsed, and stored upside down in cartons obtained from the local liquor dealers. Why upside down? To keep the dust out, of course.

Free Bottles

The sources of bottles are many and varied. Once your relatives and friends know that you are making wine, they will be happy to save you theirs, hoping to gain a few full ones for many empties. In some areas, dump-picking is a suburban art form. One can be introduced to political candidates and marriageable daughters at a really first-class dump in a chic New England village. All the very nicest people will discard their Medoc and Beaujolais jugs there. They scatter the ashy earth with empties after a Mums-sluiced debut of granddaughters. Best pickings are after Thanksgiving and the mid-winter holidays. Take your treasures home, wash well, and store.

If you frequent a restaurant catering to wine-bibers, ask the bartender to save you the fifths . . . after a suitable preamble. He may be willing to put aside what you need, if he understands that you are a wine-*maker*. Do not give him the impression that you plan to come scrounging in his trash cans with your wino cronies. An arrangement between gentlemen, with the gratuity of a bottle or two, if he loves the grape.

How to Scrounge

Not all restaurants will do this favor. Some types will tell you it is against the law, and in some states, this is, indeed, the case.

Accept all gifts with gratitude. Be prepared to discard screw-type whiskey crocks, flat-faced gin bottles, and all sizes and shapes bulbous, runty, and "cute." Expect the Chianti fiasco with the unravelled wicker base and candle wax in seventeen colors that once graced somebody's playroom bar. (Chianti is shipped from Italy to America when the local *signorini* know it is fit only to wash the pigs with. Never buy a Chianti over three years old, for this reason. The bottles are inexpensive and frail, hence the wicker, or these days, plastic base. They are hard to cork. Pretty, perhaps, but useless.) You want fifth bottles designed and made especially for red wine. They should be thick-walled, dark green in color, with heavy bases to take the impact of corking, with straight long necks to make a tight seal. One does not decant the labor of months into the silly whimsies of packaging "experts."

As soon as you collect a dozen bottles, wash them thoroughly in really *hot* water. Fill a quarter full, put your thumb over the opening, and shake vigorously. Invert to drain and store upside down.

All your corks must be new. Purchase two gross from the supplier you have been dealing with thus far, or order by mail from any of the suppliers listed in the rear pages of this book. Since they are very light, the postage will be nickels and dimes. Indicate that you are bottling *fifths* on your order. Get straight, *not* champagne, closures, which require a special corker and a tool to fix the wires. You do *not* need champagne corks to cork a champagne bottle. The plain variety will do very nicely.

Correct Corks

You will need a corker, and the simpler the better. An inexpensive variety is turned of hard wood and slotted on one side. The cork fits into this breech, like a cartridge in a rifle. A simple plunger drives the cork down a tapered metal sleeve, compressing it so that it slides neatly into the bottle neck. Once free of the sleeve, it plumps out instantly, making a perfect seal. The cost of corks and the corker should be divided, if many hands are to be at work. Otherwise, it is the

Master's purchase and his to wield, at least for demonstration purposes. The Apprentices will do the bulk of the labor, as usual.

Wash with Care

All bottles should be washed *a second time* the day before bottling begins. Each bottle should be checked against a bright, bare light bulb to make certain that no deposits, molds, dead bugs or foreign bodies lurk within. Discard any that seem at all doubtful. Use a couple of rejects for a trial-run with the corker.

A simple corker.

Bottling Techniques

Apprentice Labors

Corking bottles is considered a discipline in the *La Mancha Gustatory, Wine-Making and Folk-Dancing League,* like unto all-night vigils and prolonged fasts. For this reason, it takes place under conditions that are physically grueling. The Apprentice squats on a low rickety stool beside a steaming kettle of corks, plucks one free, scalding his fingers, feeds it into the corker, gets a filled bottle from another slavey, and drives the cork home. Hands snatch this one away for casing. More hands present another to be stoppered. Rapid work that is certain to strain backs and tempers, cause the thigh muscles to seize, the fingers to blister, and the throat to parch. One L.M.G.W.M.

& F.D.L. motto is: "A good Apprentice is always uncomfortable but never rebellious." Such monastic severities can be avoided. Try the following procedure:

1. The night before bottling, bring to the cellar a sturdy wooden table and cover it with an entire Sunday issue of the New York *Times*. This should be pressed flat with a few boards and bricks. This provides the next day's bottlers with a table at convenient height, neatly padded to cushion the slight shock of corking, well papered to absorb spills.

2. The night before bottling put all your corks into two or more large kettles to soak. Fill each kettle half-full and cover.

Steaming Corks

3. At breakfast-time on bottling day, place the cork-kettles on the stove, bring to a boil, turn down, and steam for *at least an hour*, preferably longer. Let the steam penetrate the corks, making each one soft. You should be able to squeeze one in your hand until liquid runs. Wet corks are easy to work with and never break. Dry corks will not slide easily in the sleeve of the corker, will not slide free to plump themselves in the neck of the bottle, but will stick half-way and shear, leaving a plugged corker and a half-corked bottle. Wet corks, then, well-stirred and "cooked." When they are done, carry them down to the cellar in their kettles, remove the cover on the first one and set it someplace handy. Try a cork in a reject bottle.

The Knack

4. Practice corking. There is a knack. You will soon discover that you cannot drive the cork home with your bare hand. Since wine will not compress like air, you cannot cork a bottle filled too full. You must have at least three inches of air

space. The cork, inserted, will take two inches. Fill a reject bottle with water, leaving the proper room.

5. Buy or borrow a rubber-headed mallet, to save wear and tear on your hands. Load the corker, set it on top of the bottle, and drive the cork home with two or three firm swats on the plunger-top with the mallet. The cork will resist compression somewhat, even when it has been driven almost free, that is, almost completely within the bottle. Strike the plunger down a few times sharply, then lift away the corker. Properly done, the cork will be flush with the top of the bottle. Run a few more reject bottles until you get the hang of it.

Production-Line Precision

The Master should properly deploy his man power. The Journeyman should see that the following equipment is handy:

> **Two gross, well-cooked corks in covered kettles.**
>
> **One corker.**
>
> **One rubber mallet (a hammer is a fair substitute).**
>
> **One basic siphon-set: the dowel with siphon-tube fastened in place with string, as used for racking.**
>
> **One sturdy plastic pail.**
>
> **Four gallon jugs with clean, snug-fitting screw-type closures.**
>
> **Two hundred and fifty fifth bottles, well-washed and inspected.**
>
> **Newspapers to catch spills.**
>
> **A glass for sipping, sniffing, and general admiration.**

Bottling and corking.

Man Power Use

The Journeyman keeps a steady supply of empties ready to be filled. One Apprentice runs the siphon and fills the bottles. Another Apprentice moves the "fills" to the table for corking. Yet a third man, perhaps the Master, corks. The Journeyman places the filled bottles in cartons for storage and distribution. Change jobs around after each four cases, or after every fifty bottles have been cased.

The Magic Moment

The Journeyman is deft with screwdriver and hammer by now. The wax around the bung is scraped away, the bung pried loose and lifted away. The Journeyman yields his place to the Master. Apprentices wring their hands and elbow each other. The Master adjusts his apron, steps forward, and places nose to bung-hole. He sniffs once, twice, but says nothing. He waves the siphon into position. An Apprentice giggles nervously, and his mates gag him. The Apprentice so delegated sucks on the tube, starting the suction and the wine flows into the first bottle, set inside the plastic bucket. When the first bottle is filled, the Master holds out his hand, fingers curled loosely. The Journeyman springs forward with The Glass. The Glass is filled. The Apprentice pinches the tube, holding the suction, but shutting off the flow of wine. The Master raises the glass to the light. The wine is absolutely without free sediment, a deep clear red. The Master grunts. Apprentices whinny and drool. The Master sniffs, testing for bouquet. The cool wine will not have much, but this is part of the ritual and not to be omitted.

How to "Chew" Wine

The Master sips and "chews" the wine thoughtfully. The technique to be perfected here is to make this act look *absolutely natural*. Simply, it is a combination of aeration, tongue-lolling, and gargle. Done with finesse, it suggests most dramatically a youth spent in dim, cool, monastic cellars. Sloppily executed, chewing conveys, at best, that your dentures have gone askew in mid-swallow; at worst, that you are prone to nervous fits. About a quarter of a mouthful. Open your lips slightly and inhale gently, while raising the tip of the tongue. Air will mix with the wine, but you will not choke. Close mouth and rinse. The inside of the cheeks are sensitive; you will feel the sharpness of an astringent wine. Of course, you should have no such sensation with your own lovingly-processed mouthful. Fumes and flavors should be all pleasant, all clear and youthful. Now, mere mortals are habituated to swallowing wine after tasting. A true Master, at this point, will *spit every drop into the nearest receptacle, without showing the slightest emotion.* Apprentices swoon, and even hardened Journeymen pale. Something dreadful has occurred! All that work gone for nothing? Fifty gallons of vinegar?

O.K. Words

Not so. The Master may mutter, *"Ça va, ça va,"* or *"Bene, bene!"* or perhaps a nicely modulated Lower Rhine Valley *"Hein?"* Even a thoughtful *"Ummmm!"* will do. The Master hands back the empty glass and waves his minions to their labors. (A Master receives compliments on his wine, but never praises his own product. He who owns a diamond mine never needs to advertise.)

Casing and Waxing

Fill each bottle to within three inches of the top, cork with care and place in cardboard liquor cartons. An exact and even count is maintained. Twelve bottles per case equals two and two-fifths gallons. Every five cases equals sixty bottles or

How Much in a Case?

twelve gallons. When ten cases have been filled, your barrel is half empty. If you have been careful and regular in racking and topping off, you should get twenty cases or 240 fifth bottles of superior red table wine.

Siphon with Care

Exercise the same cautions in bottling as in both rackings. Place the low end of the siphon tube about half-way down the dowel. When the suction breaks, lower the tube. Take care not to agitate the wine. Draw clear wine off the lees. Check regularly past the three-quarter mark. When the wine darkens, case the subsequent bottles separately. Finally, at the end, you will draw out heavy fluid, murky and much like the stuff you allowed to settle for topping-off. This

Screw-Type Closures

should be siphoned into clean gallon jugs, very full, and sealed with clean, *tight* screw closures. Let it sit a month. The lees will drop to the bottom of the jugs, and you can draw off and cork *most* of it. Don't be greedy. Allow for some loss through declared inferiority. If it is not so good as the rest, don't bother to bottle and cork it. It is acceptable to add to stews, and makes a good *marinade* with herbs. Consider the bottom of the barrel as cooking wine and be happy. You have learned attentiveness and patience. You have a quality product. Complete the process in style.

Test for Leaks

Test corks for soundness by tipping each case on its side, *carefully*. Let them rest so overnight. A bad cork will leak, of course, but do not panic if you discover a drop or so of wine on a cork here and there. These are minute leaks, smaller than pin-holes, and proper waxing will seal them.

Eloquent Waxing

Heat about half a box of paraffin (the kind of wax used to seal jelly jars) in a clean tin can set in a saucepan of hot water. Stir in two tablespoons of powdered artists' colors, preferably (because traditionally) red. Carry down to the cellar with pliers or hot pads and set on the floor. Take the first bottle and dip it two inches deep in the liquid, tinted wax. The bottle will be cool, and the wax will congeal at once. If the wax does not completely cover the exposed surface of the cork, dip again, or smooth it sealed with your finger. Waxing can be done as fast as one man can dip. You may need another batch of tinted paraffin. Keep the excess for next year. Replace each dipped bottle in its case.

Le Cave du Vin

A cardboard carton on its side will do to store your wine, although you run the risk of having bottles slide out and break. The cost of manufactured wine racks is prohibitive. Many are so small they only hold a dozen bottles. Admirable gifts, they will not do to store your ample stock. For about sixteen cents apiece, you can get hexagonal terra-cotta drain pipes. These stack splendidly and have an inside diameter large enough to allow easy insertion and removal of

A $40 "Cave"

even champagne bottles. Moreover, they tend to control temperatures as they shield your wine. Call it forty dollars and you have a simple, safe, and attractive cellar or "cave."

Wooden Wine Bins

Weekend carpenters and do-it-yourselfers will be tempted to build more elaborate wooden bins. Two notes of caution: make sure that the bins are built on the bias, X-shaped, to prevent bottles from rolling free to fall and shatter when you remove one; make sure that any system of bins you build is constructed of heavy lumber and reinforced with iron tie-rods. Fifty gallons of wine in bottles is *heavy!* You are binning in excess of 400 pounds of wine. Liquid, plus bottles, creates considerable crushing weight, plus a force acting against the *sides* of your bins as well. Your bins should be solid wood, well-braced. Such a structure will cost more than drain-pipes. The alternate systems are illustrated below. Note that the terra-cotta pipe is not stacked too high, so as to avoid sudden topples. About four tiers is maximum.

Homemade wine racks.

Storage and Aging

Wine should not be stored in any place that is either too warm or too cool. About sixty-five degrees is ideal, but not always easy to come by in a modern basement. A far corner may do, even a heated garage (provided a section can be closed off to prevent pilfering by the neighborhood kids

**How Cool?
How Long?**

or their envious parents). How long to age? That depends on you. Wine, from beginning to end, depends on human beings. It will improve with age up to about its third year. The Master of *La Mancha* and I have dipped bills in our '59, a powerful brew of Petit Syrrahs that is still holding its own. The more feminine vintages of the mid-sixties are gentlewomen of charm and grace, but their prime, alas, is past. Ma'mselle '65 suffered from too long exposure to heat and then disappointed all. The past two years have been superb. Frankly, among *La Manchans*, a bottle two years old is a rarity. The pleasures of the table and a rigorous program of spontaneous folk-dancing makes for ferocious thirsts. Apprentices are parched when it again comes time to bottle a given year. We have *never* been short of empty bottles.

Save-a-Case

Nevertheless, it is great fun to put aside perhaps a case per year, creating a mini-museum of your own vintages to be drunk only at high ceremonies and ritual repasts. Each dusty bottle will bring back memories of meals eaten, jokes told, song sung, and lovers kissed. Use the past to toast the present and the present to savor the past. *Sainte!*

SLIP-SKIN SQUEEZINGS

RED AND WHITE WINE FROM *VITIS LABRUSCA*

"Slip-Skins"

Although grapes suitable for wine-making are grown more widely than the novice vintner may be aware, about eighty percent of *Vitis vinifera*—the wine-grape varieties—are nurtured in California. The second most significant area of viticulture is Ohio and the third, New York. A determined Master will find one or more of the varieties listed below grown commercially in Arkansas, Delaware, Michigan, Missouri, Maryland, New Jersey, New Mexico, Oregon, Pennsylvania, Tennessee, Texas, and Washington. "Seek and ye shall find." These varieties are *Vitis labrusca,* commonly called "slip-skins." Many do not contain enough sugar to ferment to wine without the addition of sugar to the must and the use of a yeast starter. This adds one or more steps to the processing.* The purchase of sugar also adds to the total cost. For these reasons, the home

*If you have not read the preceding section you can turn to page 17 for a brief review of the steps.

vintner may wish to obtain and process smaller amounts. Information about equipment and how-to lies here, halfway between the noble clusters of the Napa Valley and the humble, roadside dandelion.

Common American Grapes

Athens. An early ripening cousin to the Concord. Needs sugar added and yeast starter.

Beta. Not well-known outside the North Plain states. Makes a strong wine that requires two years' aging to lose its sharpness. Can be made without sugar and yeast starter, but the must should be tested with a sacchrometer and read twenty percent sugar or higher.

Catawba. Available quite widely for making white wine, dry or sweet, also domestic champagne.

Concord. The famous blue slip-skin. Grows almost everywhere, including wild. Needs sugar and yeast starter.

Delaware. The best American white wine grape. Grown widely, it can be processed like a Beta and is much easier to find.

Diamond. An Ohio grape, also found around the Finger Lakes of New York and along the south shore of Lake Erie. Makes a good white wine.

Dutchess. Another fine white-wine grape, but not easy to find. Can be processed like the Delaware and Catawba.

Elvira. Another New York State grape, but found elsewhere. Needs sugar and a yeast starter. Should be drunk young.

Fredonia. Grown in the East and Southwest. For red wine, but needs sugar and yeast starter.

Herbemont. A Southern grape, grown in many states. Makes red wine.

Muscadine. Another Southern favorite. Needs sugar and yeast starter to produce a good red wine.

Niagara. Generally grown only as a table fruit. With sugar and yeast starter makes a pleasant white wine with rather "fruity" flavor.

Ontario. Another green table-fruit variety. Kin to the Niagara, it requires the same processing to make a very similar white wine.

Scuppernong. A well-known Southern variety, sometimes found wild. Requires sugar and yeast starter, sometimes only the yeast. Makes a "fruity" white wine, very pleasant when served chilled.

Yeast Starters

With *Vitis vinifera* varieties, home vintners can rely on the natural yeasts that come right with the grapes. However, home-grown or wild grapes of *Vitis labrusca* varieties may not have sufficient yeasts to ferment completely or may contain wild yeasts of the wrong kind. Therefore, when making slip-skin wine or wine from any other orchard fruit, *always use a pure strain yeast starter.*

Yeast starters minimize sediment by vigorous boiling that converts the must to its highest potential alcoholic content. Yeast starters eliminate all trace and taste of sugar, even the bulk amounts dumped and stirred into a Concord grape must. Used correctly, a yeast starter will ensure a *dry* red wine from a sickeningly-sweet, murky slip-skin must. *Follow directions with care.*

Foreign Yeast Starters

Vierka Yeast, a West German product, comes in liquid form. One bottle will allow you to process ten to twelve gallons of wine. It must be started *at the time of crushing*, then added. It comes in a number of types, Burgundy and Bordeaux for making red wine, Sauterne, Liebfraumilch, and Champagne for making whites. *Wunderbar! Follow directions with care.*

Liofermenti Yeast, an Italian product of very great efficiency, comes in a dry form, and a small bottle will make five to six gallons of wine in one flavor only: Chianti. It must be started ahead of time, then added to fermenting must. *Mama mia! Follow directions with care.*

Vinotex General Purpose Yeast Tablets come (obviously) from England. Each tablet is thriftily packaged in foil for good shelf life and will make precisely one gallon of white or red wine. It works well, but gives no flavor to wine. Very discreet. It can be added directly, but the manufacturers suggest prior starting. Don't be put off by the square name. Amateur wine-making is very big in the British Isles, complete with gold medals in annual competitions in about a dozen varieties. English fruit wines can be obtained in liquor stores catering to wine drinkers and are well worth sampling, especially the apple wines. Good show, you chaps! *Follow directions with care.*

English Fruit Wines

Montrachet Yeast is a new French product, also a dry, granulated additive in foil wrapping. Each envelope will make, curiously enough, exactly five gallons of red wine, while adding a Montrachet sniff and smack. Will also make white wine suitable for entering in all British gold medal run-offs. It alone can be added to fermenting must, *without* prior starting. Stir in sugar, add a packet, pour into five-gallon bottle, water-seal and wait. *Formidable! Follow directions with care.*

Order your choice of yeast starter from the suppliers listed in the rear section of this book. Prices are approximate. Place your order *before picking or purchasing fruit.*

Equipment for Making Five Gallons of Red or White Wine

One fruit press or potato-masher.

Two ten-gallon earthenware crocks.

One five-gallon distilled-water bottle.

One rubber stopped for water bottle, pierced to take glass tube.

Five feet of flexible rubber tubing, with inside diameter to fit tightly over glass tube inserted in stopper.

One bolt of cheesecloth.

One large pickle jar.

One sieve, large.

One colander.

One solid rubber stopper for water bottle.

White, granulated suger.

Yeast starter.

METHOD #1 FOR RED WINE

The Concord slip-skin is grown everywhere except in the Northern Plain states. The home vintner searching out grapes in a local arbor or commercial vineyard will most likely end up with Concords. The other varieties suitable for making red wine can be processed in the same way as the Concords are. White wines are treated separately in the section on making white wines, METHOD #2.

First, believe nothing that anybody tells you about Concord grape wine: that it's lousy, that it's as good as/better than California wine, that it's so sweet you just crush, ferment, and drink. Not true. What a wine made from *Vitis labrusca* tastes like depends on how you process the fruit. As Master in your own cellar, you will proceed as follows, even when convinced the measures and amounts are wrong or that these pages are misprinted. *La Mancha* vintners once scorned directions for making red wine from Concord grapes. Never again. Read and believe and prosper. The rule is this: Concord grapes and

You Better Believe!

all *Vitis labrusca* uncles, cousins, and kin are generally deficient in sugar content. They must be crushed and fermented, then *abundant sugar is added to the must.* You will need a saccharimeter and should experiment first with a small quantity of grapes, say enough to make five gallons of wine.

Pick or purchase enough Concord-type grapes to yield slightly more than five gallons of wine, about *two bushels* of ripe fruit. Crush unwashed grapes in the first ten-gallon crock. Remember the fermenting fruit will boil and create a *chapeau,* which will rise. Leave enough room for this, about one-third of the crock, or use both crocks. Crush with a hand- or electric-powered fruit press, about ten minutes' work for which you should pay no rental fee. More simply, smash each berry with an old-fashioned potato-masher or a new-fangled cole-slaw chopper. Do *not* use a Waring blender or electric mixer. Allow

A hand-powered fruit press.

Fermenting Concords

the fruit to ferment at least five days to seven days. If you have been one-crocking, bail the slop into the colander set over crock number two. Press pulp with your fist, then dump the pulp into a loose sack of cheesecloth. You will have more than five gallons of murky, sweet, somewhat fizzy-tasting must and a leaky bag of cheesecloth filled with damp pulp. Wash crock number one, set the strainer on top and bail the must into the strainer from crock number two. Got it? You have done a crude, quick job of pre-filtering. Wash crock number two and set aside to dry.

Pour enough must into the pickle jar to float

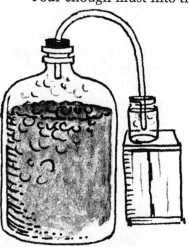

A water-seal for the five-gallon bottle.

a saccharimeter with ease and grace. It should measure about ten percent sugar in the must, possibly fifteen percent.

Adding Sugar

Add eight ounces of plain white granulated sugar per measured gallon of wine. *What? A half-pound per gallon?* Yes. Any less and you'll have five gallons of superior vinegar. *Eight ounces to a gallon of must.*

Stir until all sugar is dissolved. At least fifteen minutes, better a half hour. When you feel the bottom of the crock, you should have no sensation of granules, touch no sunken sugar-reefs.

Take the sack of cheesecloth filled with pressed pulp. Wring it smartly, forcing out juice. Tie up the loose end with string and let it hang over the crock and drip overnight or for twenty-four hours. Untie and toss in the garbage can.

Adding Yeast

Now add yeast starter, having followed all directions in preparing or measuring it for five gallons of wine.

The sugar-strengthened must should be boiling again. Pour it into the five-gallon distilled-water bottle, set the rubber stopper firmly in place, connect the hose to the glass tube and place the loose end of the tubing deep in your pickle jar, filled with water.

Unlike the water-seal on a fifty-gallon wooden barrel holding *Vitis vinifera* must, through which carbonic acid gas imperceptibly seeps, this simple fermentation-lock will have to handle a regular, if decreasing, bubbly escape of gas. *Check the pickle jar once each day, making certain the tube end is beneath the water surface.* Top-off.

When the action shows and stops, a good portion of the wine will have fined itself. The yeast starter will convert all of the sugar to alcohol. You will not have a sweet red wine, unless you stop the fermentation too soon. Sacramental red wine from Concord grapes is arrested before it finishes fermenting, that's all.

Rack or Ruin?   Rack, of course. Unstopper the five-gallon bottle. Siphon the clear wine off the dregs into a clean crock. Wash out the five-gallon bottle and pour the wine back in. Re-stopper, set the tube back in the pickle jar and wait another week or so. Take care to top-off when you rack, just as for the *Vitis vinifera* process. Usually one racking is enough. Siphon the wine into bottles, cork, and wax. *Voila!*

METHOD #2 FOR WHITE WINE

Processing *Vitis labrusca* grapes into white wine is somewhat more complicated than making any sort of red. All procedures must be carefully observed. Try to use Catawba, Delaware, Diamond, Dutchess, Elvira, Ontario, or Scuppernong varieties. Niagara, only if you cannot obtain the others.

The First Rule The rule here is, regardless of type of grape used, *the juice must not be fermented on the skins.*

Pick or purchase two bushels of grapes, enough for five gallons. Buy or have your lady make a cloth bag big enough to hold one bushel, and let this bag be of clean, strong, *unstarched* cloth and let the seams be double-stitched and reinforced.

You will need your wine press. Put one bushel or less into the bag, set the bag in the basket of the press, put the plate on top, having first smoothed out the loose cloth. Press *slowly,* allowing the juice to run into a plastic bucket. Back the press off, stir the grapes around, and press again. Repeat this process three times. Discard the pulp and repeat this process with the rest of the fruit. Pour the juice into a ten-gallon crock, dip your pickle jar full, and measure the sugar content with your sacchrometer.

24% Sugar

Add enough sugar to bring the measured amount up to *a reading of twenty-four percent sugar.* This will be about half a pound of sugar to a gallon of juice.

Pour sugar-strengthened juice into a five-gallon distilled-water bottle, Reserve excess. You may need some for your yeast starter. You will need some for topping-off. Do not stopper.

Let the must work for several days. It will look *awful,* and spew froth and impurities that will drool down the sides of the bottle and cause the fastidious to blench and turn aside. Ignore them. When the major violence seems to have stopped, in about five to seven days, you will note a steady bubbling up of whitish beads. Top-off regularly during the period of boiling. On the last day, the level of liquid should have lowered about two inches down in the neck. Plug with rubber stopper, attach tubing, and put the tube end in your pickle jar filled with water to make a safe seal. Allow it to ferment overnight or for twenty-four hours.

Adding Tannin

You must add tannin to the wine at this point. Buy dry tannic acid at a drug store. You will need only *one gram* per five gallons. Siphon from the bottle about a quart, dissolve the gram in it, pour the must back into the bottle, stir with a dowel and reseal.

A Slowness

Once the white wine must is again under water-seal, you must wait and wait. After thirty days in which you carefully keep the pickle jar filled, rack the wine into a ten-gallon crock, wash the sediment from the five-gallon bottle, pour the wine back, and re-seal. Wait another thirty days. Repeat racking. This time stopper the bottle *without water-seal*. Use a rubber stopper or a tight-fitting cork, well-smeared with paraffin. Make sure the cork or stopper is airtight. Wait another thirty days and rack a *third* time. The wine should be medium to dry, clear as crystal and ready for bottling, corking, and sipping. Do not hurry white wine. The rule of thumb is: press in October one year, bottle 365 days later. One full year to make one fine wine.

Rack Three Times

A Trick of the Trade

You cannot get the varieties of grape listed earlier? You are a Master Vintner beset. Concords, Concords everywhere and not a dram of Delaware. Do not fret. You can make white wine from red or dark-skinned *Vitis labrusca* fruit quite easily. Why, it happens every day, in the very best of cellars!

White Wine from Red Grapes

Pick, purchase, and press Concords or other dark-skinned grapes exactly as for white wine. Use one bushel or less at a time inside a stout, clean cloth bag, press slowly, stir the pulp around in the bag, then press again. Discard pulp and repeat with another bushel of grapes.

After pressing, allow to ferment for five to seven days. Prepare yeast starter, according to directions. Measure juice with saccharimeter and *add sugar to twenty-four percent.* Mix in the yeast starter. Pour into five-gallon water bottle. Rack once.

Animal Charcoal

NOW. Allow the wine to sit for thirty days after the first racking. Buy *five grams* of purified "animal charcoal" at a drug store. Rack the wine a second time. When the wine has been siphoned into the ten-gallon crock, mix in the charcoal. Animal charcoal is made from bones, not wood. Animal charcoal in this amount will absorb all the color from the wine. In time. Recork the bottle and let it sit for sixty days, or until the wine goes clear. The animal charcoal will settle slowly to the bottom of the bottles. Siphon the clear wine off the lees, bottle, and cork.

The Master Vintner: A Dramatic Interlude

An industrious Master seeking total dominance over his unruly cellar-squad will make five gallons of white wine in silent secrecy. When the Journeyman shows up two weeks before Columbus Day to whang the hoops down on the fermenters and aging casks and fill all with water for tightening the seams, the Master has a small but delicious surprise. The Chief Troglodyte is out in the yard playing with the hose, like the overgrown kid he is. Perhaps the labors that lie within the rather limited range of trust the Master has set for him now extends as far as sulphuring the aging casks. So much the better. Pride goeth before a fall.

The Master appears from the dim depths holding a bottle and opener. His lady fetches a wine glass. The Journeyman gapes and applies claws to some hairy portion of himself. Bewildered though he is, he hates to admit it. No Apprentice he! Dialogue ensues as follows:

> **Journeyman: Hey, Your Excellency, whatcha got there, huh?**

Master: Oh, this? Why, just one bottle of vin blanc . . .

Journeyman: Wheredyuhbuyit?

Master (with a light laugh): Oh, you can't buy it . . .

Journeyman: Jeez. Wheredyuhswipeit?

Master (drawing the cork): There are twenty-four bottles more in the cave.

Journeyman (aghast): Highjacked?

Master (very quietly, accepting the glass from his lady): I made it.

Journeyman (stunned): No foolin'!

Master (crisply): No, and no Vitis vinifera either, you hirsute oaf. This is a Labrusca Liebfraumilch . . . nothing really special. Just an amusing little white I ran off from some slip-skins I picked up locally. Try some, my dear.

Master hands glass to Lady, who sips, smiles, and flushes prettily.

Lady: Your Excellency, you must enter this in the British Isles Home Wine-makers Gold Medal Contest! First prize is yours, assured by your own combination of savoir-faire, sugar, yeast-starters and plain old common-sense!

Master (demurring): My dear, you go too far. A gram of tannin here, a smidgin of animal charcoal there. Follow Directions with Care and . . .

Lady (passionately, heedless of the gaping Journeyman, who is tormented by envy and desire): And I am yours forever!

Lady kisses Master in a near-frenzy, Journeyman tugs his forelock, scuffs his clumsy foot on the ground and looks away. After a moment, he dares to clear his throat.

Master (gently disengaging): Forever? Why not? You age, my love, like the finest Burgundy.

Lady: Gee! You say the sweetest things, Your Excellency! . . .

Master: Yes, I do. Incidentally, I believe one of the children has impaled himself amongst the Florabunda bushes. Why not have a look-see, while I share a glass with . . . with . . . (struggles to recall the Journeyman's name) . . . this . . . fellow, here?

Lady exits. The Master decants a dollop of deliciousness and the Journeyman, clumsily aping his betters, sniffs, chews, and swallows, the latter act with ill-concealed greed. He wipes his lips with the back of his cleaner hand.

Journeyman: Say! Hey, that's really . . .

Master: Not difficult at all. If you just Follow Directions with Care. Do get on with it, now, old fellow, won't you?

Journeyman: Boy, wait till I tell them stupid Apprentices about this!

Master: Do just that. After the barrels have been made ready, of course.

Journeyman: Oh, Jeez, of course. Yeah, sure, right! I'll get right to . . .

The Master has slipped away down into his cellar, taking the bottle with him, naturally. A tranquil afternoon lies before him, applying labels perhaps, his tongue moistened with slip-skin sec. He has taken care to provide himself with another glass. His Lady will gladly find and wash the one left above . . . if the Journeyman does not break it first, which happens, alas, from time to time. He is, poor devil, not quite the stuff a Master Vintner is made of. Or born of.

HOME FRUIT WINES

MAKING WINE FROM FRUITS

Summer and Winter Wines

Although *Vitis labrusca* varieties of grapes are grown, as we have seen, in every state in the union—either commercially or for personal consumption—they are all seasonal fruits. Depending on climate, they ripen between late August and mid-October. However, it is possible to make certain types of wine in early summer or mid-winter, even year-round.

It is not possible to make a dry wine from most fruits or vegetables. The wines listed in this section will be medium to sweet, good dessert wines, pleasant tipples "on the rocks," or with a splash of soda. Do not try to drink them with roast meat or fowl. Do try cider wine with ham. The contrast of flavors makes each more interesting.

5 Gallons Each

All recipes are calculated to make five gallons of wine. Plan ahead for bottles, since you will most likely wish to keep them separate from bottles used for *Vitis vinifera* or *Vitis labrusca* grapes. Why five gallons? It is easier to make a ton of steel than one and half pounds of steel, no? Does any cook bake three-sevenths of any sort of

A 10-Gallon Crock

pie? Can anybody bake a single slice of bread? With a ten-gallon earthenware crock to ferment juices in, you are assured of having room enough in it for more than five gallons. Remember, you need extra must for topping-off. Five gallons are twenty-five bottles. Subtract the one sipped empty by a thirsty corking crew and you have exactly two cases. Since not all people relish sweet or medium-sweet wines, two cases are likely to be enough both for consumption and holiday giving.

Yeast Starters, Again

You will be starting fermentation with yeast, and for home fruit wines, the cheapest, most satisfactory yeast is plain old Fleishman's. One pressed cake or one packet for every five to seven gallons of juice. A simple proportion to remember and one that will produce a vigorous boil, assuring, in turn, that all fruit sugars and added sugars will convert to alcohol.

Some Hints, Cautions, and Reminders

Ferment in your ten-gallon crock, never in an aluminum kettle or any other receptacle made of metal. Skim the surface and strain all liquids before they go into your five-gallon distilled-water bottle.

Keep some juice in reserve for topping-off. You need at least six gallons of must to make five gallons of bottled delight. Keep surplus in clean, tightly-capped gallon jugs or screw-topped quarts for easy handling.

Before stoppering to make a water-seal, lower the liquid in the neck of the five-gallon bottle about two inches. While too much air is the assassin of wine, some is needed to complete fermentation.

Hot paraffin should be smeared over all junctures after you remove the water-seal and close the five-gallon bottle with a solid stopper of snug cork.

Whenever you add sugar, make certain that you stir the strengthened fruit juice thoroughly, for at least fifteen minutes.

Some "Nevers" to Know

Never add yeast to hot liquids. Never add yeast cake or dry granules to liquid in the five-gallon bottle. Always put yeast in the crock to start the juices.

Be prepared to fine most of these wines. A standard system for this is: Dissolve three grams of pure leaf gelatin in a quart of wine siphoned from the five-gallon bottle. Allow this to stand overnight. Return the liquid to the big bottle, stir for five minutes with a dowel. Re-stopper and seal with wax. The gelatin will settle to the bottom, taking sediment and particles of unfermented fruit pulp with it. The beauty of the five-gallon distilled-water bottle is that you can see the fining process and therefore are not tempted to bottle and cork until your eyes tell you that the wine has gone clear.

How to "Fine" Wine

Store home fruit wines in a cool place. Most of these can be chilled before serving.

More heroic brews can be made by adding a fifth bottle of a brandy made from the same fruit your wine is made from: Laird's Applejack to five gallons of cider or apple wine, for instance, or a fifth of apricot brandy to your apricot wine. This is not cheating; it is fortifying. A wine thus fortified should keep forever. The taste is improved, but the percentage of alcohol is not really raised that much. You will still have a wine, not a fruit liqueur.

Fortifying Fruit Wines

All measurements of additives—sugar, gelatin, etc.—are exact. Have your druggist weigh out grams for you on his scale to insure precision.

RECIPES FOR HOME FRUIT WINES

Cider Wine

Use only that kind of cider to which *no preservatives* have been added. In it, thoroughly dissolve two pounds of sugar for each gallon of cider. Normally, it will ferment by itself. You may add half a cake of pressed yeast or half an envelope. **Away with Froth** Skim the froth from the surface of the crock and bail the cider through cheesecloth on its way to the five-gallon bottle. Vigorous fermenting is usually complete in three days. Keep under water-seal for about a week, then stopper the bottle until the wine fines itself. Cider wine, *mirabile dictu*, normally doesn't need to be racked. It can be drunk as soon as it is clear, say two weeks after being stoppered. This makes it available for adult Halloween sipping.

Apple Wine

Apples are in supermarkets nearly all year long. Processing them into wine is a slow, rather messy job. This wine will come out clear, brilliantly so, and will not have a cloying taste. The entire process will use up one of those awful

spring vacations when the kids are out of school and it rains too much for them to play outside. The Master can supervise this one, turning all labor over to his *Frau* and up to a half-dozen restless "What'll-we-do-*now?*" sub-Apprentices.

Look up a fruit wholesaler in the phone book and get a price on a few bushels of Macintosh or Red Delicious apples. Stop by the nearest Woolworth or J.C. Penny and invest in an adequate supply of paring knives and a box of Band-aids. Cover the cellar floor with newspapers, gather the troops and announce: "For the rest of the week we shall make *Hochfeinste Auslese Apfelwein!*" (Hoke'-fine-stir Ow'-slayser Ap'-fell-vine).

Drinken-Sie Deutsch?

Apples must be cored, crudely, some of the seeds removed, and the fruit cut into small pieces. The small pieces should be dumped into one ten-gallon earthenware crock and chopped fine with a cole-slaw chopper. While the kids are up to this, run up a double-seamed cloth bag of plain, un-starched cotton cloth. No, an old pillowcase will *not* do at all. The Junior Journeyman can switch from cole-slaw chopper to potato-masher or food-mill, but firmly deny access to any electric-powered devices unless you were planning on re-painting the cellar over the weekend, anyway. The apples should be pulped as fine as you can get this work done. The finer the pulp, the easier the

Strainer-Bags

pressing. You may wish to use a conventional grape-crusher, once the cored apples are in small pieces.

Place the pulp in the bag, put the bag in the basket of the press, and press slowly. Back the press off and tumble the pulp around by hand several times. With time and effort, you can extract all the usable juice. Coring, seeding, chopping, pulping, and pressing can take an entire afternoon, even a whole day. Everybody has some piece of the action, yet it is a group project. Delightfully sloppy and sweet and sticky, too.

Let the juice run into a clean plastic pail, while the crock used for chopping is washed clean. Pour the juice into the crock, measuring it, until you have seven gallons. (It is very likely that you will need more apples. Juice content per bushel is hard to figure. Some apples some years in some seasons are very juicy, other kinds, other times, much less so. Several trips to the wholesaler will give everyone something to do.) Let the juice stand for several hours or overnight. Strain it through cheesecloth into ten-gallon crock number two.

How Much is a Bushel?

Sugar: A Rule-of-Thumb

For each gallon of liquid, add two pounds of sugar. Stir as you add, all sub-Apprentices taking turns. This part of the process will take the better part of two hours, since you are adding in excess of ten pounds of sugar. Either Master or Mom is in charge of quality-control here. There should be no sugar on the bottom of the crock at all, and no grainy feel to the liquid. Stir and stir and stir. Then about another thirty minutes of stirring.

Add one cake of yeast or one envelope. Stir this in thoroughly, too. Cover the crock with cheesecloth and pop everybody into bed early.

There will be muscle fatigue from all that biceps-building exercise.

Pray for clear weather. It will take about four days for the boiling to begin, work well, and then slow. Skim off the sludge and strain the liquid through cheesecloth into a five-gallon bottle. Water-seal. The wine will continue to ferment for three more days.

Siphon off one quart of liquid, now a rather pleasant, fizzy "hard" cider of sorts. All workers get a taste. Stir half an ounce cream of tartar into what they don't drink, pour all back into the bottle, top-off with excess liquid, and water-seal again.

Apple wine tends to work itself clear quite rapidly. Actually, the juice was pre-filtered by the cloth bag, then passed through cheesecloth on its way to the bottle after a hefty jolt of yeast to assure a vigorous boiling. You can do either one of two things at this point or, if you like, both. (There are not many life-situations these days that offer that sort of choice. Consider this subterranean wisdom for a moment. When was the last time you could choose to do one thing, the other or both . . . without running any sort of risk *Hmmm*.) Siphon off a pint for sampling. Sip and ponder. Now you know what it is like to dwell on the slopes of Olympus, for the power of the gods is, briefly, yours.

Masters Choice

You may add at this point, depending on the clarity of the wine, two and a half grams of pure leaf gelatin to whatever you have left of your siphoned pint, returning this mixture to the bottle and stirring with a dowel. You may siphon off another pint and top off with a fifth of apple brandy. You may do both. Either way, you're a winner, for the wine is bound to improve.

Allow the wine to clarify, then bottle, cork, and celebrate. You have two cases of *Hochfeinste Auslese Apfelwein.* You have provided a basic lab-session in chemistry to the kids, made it through another spring vacation without running amok, and toyed with fate in the most benign manner. Ladies have demonstrated "Women's Lib" below-stairs and gentlemen have again demonstrated what it means to be Master Vintner.

Blueberry Wine

Mid-summer manipulations produce an unusual sweet wine ready to drink in January. Here is another superb kid-occupier; somebody has got to pick five gallons of blueberries. (They can be purchased wholesale by the crate, but in many areas the fruit grows wild.)

Since this is "stoop-labor," the gathering of the fruit should be the kiddies' task. It will take days and days, since you need perhaps a half-million wild berries. Actually, they can quit or run out of fruit earlier. Just adjust the recipe down. It makes for nice little math problems.

Let us assume that some gang of miniature *brazeros* have gathered the full amount, five gallons of blueberries. (They will be an exotic crew. Who else in the neighborhood has indigo children?) Boil one gallon of water for each gallon of fruit. Put the berries into a ten-gallon earthenware crock and pour the boiling water over. Let stand overnight. The berries will swell and burst or become softened so that pressing is sloppy but a cinch. Use a clean cloth bag, press

Measure for Measure

and tumble, press again in small amounts, extracting all the liquid. Measure the juice as it goes back into the crock. Stir in three pounds of sugar for each measured gallon. Add a cake of yeast or one package of dried yeast and stir. Cover with cheesecloth to keep out the flies and go do something else that's fun for three days. If still boiling, let it go another two days.

After three to five days' fermenting, strain through cheesecloth into a bottle, water-seal, and let rest. (Shrewd Daddies and Moms will have figured out by now that berry-picking-to-fermenting will just about take care of all empty hours of a conventional summer vacation. True. The strained, fermented juice can be put in clean, tightly-capped gallon jugs and station-wagoned back home, then poured into the family five-gallon bottle.)

For some reason not quite known, it takes blueberry wine a long, slow time to fine itself and no additive seems to help much. Just be patient and make sure the water-seal does not run dry on you. Remove the water-seal on Halloween and stopper the bottle. It should be ready to drink sometime in January, just about when the kids have forgotten all about it. Surprise!

All's Well that Ends Well

Cherry Wine

Back in the days when everything was much younger and the majority of dreams were still untried, American males quaffed rum from Barbados, such lethal concoctions as "Whistle-

Belly Vengeance," and cursed the British. Ladies were not so political; the Daiquiri had not yet been invented, and only whores drank gin. A feminine favorite of colonial days was "Cherry Bounce," which, if taken liberally, made bundling-boards and other restraining devices an absolute necessity. Cherries are still sold at roadside stands by children who can't make change from a dollar bill, and the fruit has a long season, thanks to modern storage, in supermarkets and wholesale houses. Buy from somebody five gallons of fruit for cherry wine.

"I Gave My Love a Cherry..."

Mash five gallons of ripe cherries in a ten-gallon crock. Do not break the pits. Add one gallon of water for each gallon of fruit. Add one cake of pressed yeast or one envelope of dried yeast. Allow fruit and water to ferment for three to five days. Using a clean, strong, unstarched cloth bag to contain the pulp, press and tumble carefully and slowly until the liquid is extracted.

Add three pounds of sugar for each gallon of fermented juice. Stir in an ounce of cream of tartar. Stir all around well and strain through cheesecloth into a five-gallon bottle. Pick over the pressed pulp and find about four dozen unbroken pits. Drop them into the bottle and set the water-seal in place. Some home vintners crush the pits with pliers before adding, others don't. Either way, they make the final product a bit more tart.

Slow Stuff

Another slow wine to clarify itself. Allow at least thirty days under water-seal, *at least four months* before bottling. Again, you can fortify this with a bottle of cherry brandy, but do so with the understanding that you will make the wine sweeter as well as stronger. Either way, there will be plenty of bounce to every ounce.

Peach Wine

Peaches, too, can be found in markets long before and after their normally short season. This wine calls for less fruit than others, but still makes a pleasant dessert wine and is easily made.

Dissolve eight pounds of sugar in six gallons

Cream of Tartar of warm water. Add half an ounce cream of tartar and let stand for twenty-four hours. Stone four dozen ripe peaches, chop them into pieces about as big as the tip of your little finger, and add to the sugar-water mixture. Break a dozen peach pits with a vise and add them to the contents of your crock. Let stand forty-eight hours. If fermentation is not underway, add half a cake of pressed yeast or half of an envelope, stirring in well. Fermentation should take five to eight days from when you add the fruit to the sugar-water mixture, less if yeast is used.

Using a clean, strong, unstarched cloth bag to hold the sloppy fruit, press it all in one batch, allowing the juices to run into a clean plastic pail. Strain this juice through cheesecloth into your crock, then re-strain the whole batch into your five-gallon distilled-water bottle. Keep the excess in a clean, tightly-capped gallon jug for topping-off. When the juices froth, which can happen overnight, set the water-seal. The wine will continue to ferment but rather slowly. When the

Clear or Fine

action has subsided, remove the seal and stopper. Keep an eye on it from this point on. It should start to clear itself. After two months, rack it into the crock, then back into the washed bottle. Let it sit another thirty days. If needed, fine with three grams of pure leaf gelatin dissolved in one quart of wine. (See SOME HINTS, CAUTIONS, AND REMINDERS.) Again, you may choose to add one quart of peach brandy to fortify your wine. Try it first. You may like it "as is."

Raisin Wine

Raisins are grapes, of course, dried in the sun to evaporate the water and to concentrate the sugar. Raisin wine is an all-season wine, for just this reason. It, too, is rather simple to make.

Chop six pounds of raisins or run them in small lots through an electric blender. Place the chopped fruit in a ten-gallon crock. Add the rind of six lemons and the juice of one dozen. Pour over all this six pounds of sugar. Boil six gallons of water for ten minutes, turn down the heat to simmer, and carefully skim anything floating on the surface. In a country as large as ours, the

Watch that H$_2$O

quality of water varies enormously, and many urban areas "treat" water with chlorine and other substances. De-treat treated water. If you like, buy six gallons of bottled spring water and just bring it to a boil.

Add the hot water to the contents of the crock and stir constantly for an hour. When the mixture is lukewarm, add half a cake of pressed yeast or half of an envelope of dried yeast. Cover the crock with newspaper and stir it twice daily with a stick for seven days.

Bail the pulp into a clean, strong, unstarched cloth bag set in your press, discarding the lemon peels. Press the juice into a pail, then strain it into the crock through cheesecloth. Re-strain all the liquid into a five-gallon bottle, keeping the reserve in a clean, tightly-capped jug.

Water-seal and allow fermentation to run its course. Rack into a crock, wash the bottle, return the wine, and stopper the bottle. When the wine is completely clear, bottle it, cork, and start sipping.

An ideal wine for those trapped in small apartments. You have no bulk fruit to handle and need no special equipment. Not even a press. You can simply bail the raisin pulp into a cloth bag, wring it firmly (like the landlord's neck), and then allow it to drip overnight into the crock, before straining into a five-gallon bottle.

High-Rise Honey Wine

Another one for apartment dwellers with more time on their hands than room for their elbows.

Pour three gallons of boiling water over three gallons of honey in a ten-gallon crock. Stir until both are well mixed and the combination is lukewarm. Add half a cake of pressed yeast or half of an envelope of dry yeast. Cover with a newspaper and allow to ferment for about five days. Strain the mixture through cheesecloth into a five-gallon bottle, reserve the excess in a clean, tightly-capped gallon jug. Water-seal the bottle. Wait two weeks, topping-off as needed. Remove the water-seal and stopper. The gestation period is that of the human animal: nine months. This is such a pleasant little fellow that I think you will not mind waiting for him. He fines nicely, if slowly, and should require no racking at all.

**Dandelion
Wine**

**The Dandelion
Myth**

I have heard (and told) a fair amount of lies in my lifetime. A surprisingly large number have dealt with this absolutely fantastic wine somebody's Aunt Elsie used to concoct out of a handful of backyard weeds. A veritable *amontillado* according to one myth, a nectar to be preferred above the finest white Rhines according to another. I never really believe that sort of story. I have tasted a number of dandelion brews in my day, some of them quite pleasant. Not one poses a serious threat to the great wines of Germany, France, Italy, or America.

Pick five gallons of dandelion blossoms. Remove the stems, *all of them.* Pop them into a ten-gallon crock, pressing them down firmly. Add five gallons of boiling water. Let the blossoms steep for about fifteen minutes. Bail the flowers into a clean, strong, unstarched cloth bag and press well in two batches to get all the juice and color. Pour the juice back into the crock. Add half a cake of pressed yeast or half an envelope of dry yeast, stirring well. Mix together five pounds of sugar and half a cup of cheap brandy per gallon of liquid. More simply, stir in twenty pounds of sugar and one quart of cheap brandy. Allow to ferment for seven days. Skim the surface and strain through cheesecloth into a five-gallon distilled-water bottle. Let stand overnight, then water-seal. This wine should not require racking. As soon as it is clear, wait another week, just to be sure, then bottle and cork it. This is a wine to drink young, since it is not likely to improve much with age. The brandy ensures its durability and fortifies the strength.

Dent de Lion

Not a great wine, to be sure, but what book on making wines at home could possibly be considered complete without this old favorite? Dandelion wine is a triumphant conquest of a rampant weed. Other home-owners poison dandelions or slash them to death with a variety of sharp instruments. Don't do this. Pick the blossoms, add the tender young leaves to salads, boil the mature leaves with finely chopped onions and a bit of salt pork or bacon for a little "Suburban Soul-Food." Drink and eat, but do not damn that friend of mankind, that golden-frilled little nuisance the French long ago named "lion's tooth," *dent de lion*. The English corrupted the pronunciation, but it was Yankee housewives who first fermented the blooms. Bring your guests *au courant* with these fascinating bits of etymology and folk-history as you bend gracefully to pour them a second glass of pale, shimmering, scented gold. *Merci, dent de lion.*

APPENDIX

**License
Wine-Maker**

Before making wine, you must obtain duplicate copies of Form 1541, "Registration for Production of Wine for Family Use," from the office of the Alcohol and Tobacco Tax Division of the Bureau of Internal Revenue located in the division where you live. Apply in writing to the Assistant District Commissioner of the Division. Allow several weeks for the exchange of papers. By law, you must file your application, in duplicate, *five days prior* to making wine. Regional Offices of the Alcohol and Tobacco Tax Division:

**55 Tremont Street, Boston, Massachusetts
90 Church Street, New York, New York
128 North Broad Street, Philadelphia,
Pennsylvania
Peachtree-Seventh Building, Atlanta, Georgia
Faller Building, 8th & Walnut, Cincinnati, Ohio
Post Office Box 1144, Chicago, Illinois
Court House Building, Dallas, Texas
2800 Federal Building, Kansas City, Missouri
708 Minnesota Building, St. Paul, Minnesota**

Post Office Box 177, Denver, Colorado
Custom House Building, San Francisco,
California

You may be informed that in addition to a
Federal registration you are *also* required to file
an application for permission with your *state*
government. Make certain to check on this. Take
care of the necessary paperwork well in advance.

Equipment List for Wine-Making		
	Barrels	Fifty gallon size, made of charred oak, used for distilling whiskey or brandy. To manufacture fifty gallons of wine, you need two barrels for fermenting and one or two for aging.
	Bottle caps	Screw-on closures for gallon jugs. Many hardware stores carry them. Order by the gross from any bottle manufacturer.
	Bottles	Five one-fifth bottles needed for each gallon of wine. Obtain from dumps, friends, and restaurants.
	Brushes	A scrub brush is essential for cleaning barrels and crocks. A long-handled bottle brush is a great help in cleaning fifths.
	Bungs	Buy them by the dozen anywhere barrels are sold. Keep a supply on hand.
	Carboy	Another name for a five-gallon or ten-gallon glass bottle. Buy from any distilled water company or laboratory-supply house.

Corking machine	Purchase from wine-supply houses. Order when purchasing corks.
Corks	Obtain size nine, one-and-a-half inch long corks from wine-supply houses. Order in large amounts and well in advance.
Crock	Available in various sizes. Make certain what you buy or borrow is big enough (ten-gallon crock to make five gallons of wine, fifteen-gallon crock to make ten gallons). Always buy earthenware or stoneware, never use a metal pail or kettle.
Funnel	As big as you can get at the local hardware or five-and-ten. For filling barrels. Wine-supply houses carry large sizes, with inset filter. A good investment.
Jugs	Gallon jugs are needed to store excess juices and wine used in topping-off. Available at drugstores and hardware stores.
Labels	Simple gummed labels for type of fruit and date. For large-scale production, have a local printer run off several hundred.
Measuring cup	Get the quart size of plastic or glass.
Potato masher	For crushing small amounts of fruit. Cole-slaw chopper is

		handy, too. Obtain at five-and-ten.
	Saccharimeter	Obtain from wine-supply or laboratory-supply houses. A must purchase item.
	Siphon	Buy five to ten feet of rubber tubing, with a quarter-inch inside diameter. Tie to four feet of quarter-inch wood doweling to make a siphon.
	Strainer, sieve	You can profitably use two, about the same size, one coarse, the other fine wire mesh. Buy at the supermarket.
Some Chemicals Used in Wine-Making	Charcoal (animal)	Buy at drug stores. For clarifying white wines.
	Cream of tartar	Buy at drug or grocery stores.
	Soda, baking	Buy at supermarket. For cleaning barrels and casks.
	Sugar	For raising the sugar content in slip-skin and fruit wine-making. Buy in bulk, not a pound at a time.
	Sulphur	Some drug and hardware stores carry the stick-type needed to purify casks. If not, order from wine-supply house.
	Tannic acid	Used in making white wines. Buy in grams, and have the druggist measure on his scale.
	Tannin	Same as tannic acid.
	Yeast	Pure natural grape yeast

starters are available only from wine-supply houses. Baking yeasts can be purchased from the supermarket for fermenting fruit wines.

Hand- and Electric-Powered Crushers, Wine Presses

The novice wine-maker is advised to rent basic crushing and pressing equipment from persons already making wine, who are usually well-known to fruit wholesalers. Small fruit presses can be obtained at antique stores, agriculture equipment manufacturers, or farmers' supply houses.

Many wine-supply houses carry some, if not all, types of heavy equipment. Select from the list of these establishments and write requesting a catalogue.

Fruit Crushers and Grinders (Manufacturers)

Bucklein Manufacturing Co., 3765 San Rafael Avenue, Los Angeles, California (Grape crushers). The Enterprise Manufacturing Co., of Pennsylvania, Dauphin & Third Street, Philadelphia, Pennsylvania.

Hocking Valley Manufacturing Co., 1864 Alfred Avenue, Lancaster, Ohio.

Fruit and Cider Presses

G.H. Alten Co., Lancaster, Ohio.

D & B Press Co., Inc., 382 West Water Street, Syracuse, New York.

Hocking Valley Manufacturing Co., 1864 Alfred Avenue, Lancaster, Ohio.

New Jersey Agricultural Works, Trenton, New Jersey.

Stuber & Kuck, 1937 Donnel Street, Peoria, Illinois.

Grape Presses

The Enterprise Manufacturing Co. of Pennsylvania, Dauphin & Third Street, Philadelphia, Pennsylvania.

Savoy Press Manufacturing Co., 1215 Wood Street, Philadelphia, Pennsylvania.

Wine-Supply Houses

Milan Laboratory, 57 Spring Street, New York, New York. (Carries all basic equipment: presses, crushers, screw-type closures, corkers, corks, bungs, funnels, filtering equipment, saccharimeters, sulphur strips, hoop drivers, bottle brushes, etc., etc. plus all basic *chemicals*).

Semplex of U.S.A., Box 7208, Minneapolis, Minnesota 55412. (Carries all basic equipment: excellent bottle-cleaning devices, brushes, excellent European siphoning equipment; specializes in *pure strain wine yeasts* and clarifiers. Also has juice concentrates for wine-making, and small [five-, ten-, fifteen-gallon] charred white oak barrels.

Both firms are excellent houses, purveying quality equipment, materials, and supplies. Good catalogues, expert service, and advice. Each house is justly famous among home wine-makers.